From Away – Immigration to Effective Workplace Integration
By Jeanne Martinson, MA
Copyright 2016 Jeanne Martinson

Wood Dragon Books
www.wooddragonbooks.com
P.O. Box 1216, Regina, Saskatchewan, Canada S4P3B4
Telephone +1.306.569.0388

ISBN: 978-0995334212

First Printing: October 2016
Second Printing: February 2017

From Away

Immigration
to
Effective Workplace Integration

Jeanne Martinson, MA

WOOD DRAGON BOOKS

DEDICATION

This book is dedicated to my family.

First to my husband, Malcolm, for his encouragement and nudging.
Secondly, to my sister, Laurelie, for her helpful input.
Thirdly, to all my sisters - Joy, Judy, Jennifer, Laurelie – for their love
and support (through not only this book project,
but the eight before as well).

Table of Contents

Note From the Author 3
Introduction 7
How We Think 9
    Eastern Western Thinking 17
Canada's Immigration Roots 25
    Understanding the India-Pakistan Divorce 31
    From India and Pakistan to Canada 37
    From China to Canada... 43
    From Philippines to Canada 47
Religions of New Immigrants 53
    Catholicism 57
    Islam 61
    Hinduism... 65
    Sikhism 69
    Chinese Religion 73
Recruiting
    Decoding the Resume of the New Immigrant 79
    The Interview – Looking Beyond the Obvious 83
Retaining and Engaging
    Communicating (Low/High Context) 91
    Evaluating (Direct/Indirect Negative Feedback) 99
    Leading (Egalitarian/Hierarchical)........................... 107
    Deciding (Consensual/Top-down).............................. 115
    Trusting (Task/Relationship Based) 121
    Disagreeing (Confrontational/Avoid Confrontation) 129
    Scheduling (Linear/Flexible time) 137
Language 145
So What About Africa? 153
Conclusion... 157
Notes 159

Acknowledgements 161
About the Author 163

1
NOTE FROM THE AUTHOR

In 2005, I wrote the book, *War and Peace in The Workplace*. The book gave two arguments for why workplace diversity is a good idea. One, it creates a representative workplace that reflects the organization's stakeholders and Canada's population at large. Secondly, it blesses an organization with the unique talents and perspectives that diverse employees bring to the workplace.

Those two arguments no longer need to be made. In Canada, most managers are well aware that a diverse workforce is good business. The current challenge is that organizations that hire a diverse workforce may be only receiving half of the benefit of that diversity. The true virtue of a diverse workforce comes only when those diverse individuals who bring skills and abilities to an organization are used at the top level of their talent. Hiring immigrants is not the answer – or at least not the whole answer – maximizing their effectiveness, productively, and longevity is.

This book is written for managers and leaders who have struggled with understanding the newest immigration wave and how to move from merely hiring immigrants to effectively integrating them into the workplace.

This book focuses on the four top source countries of immigrants to Canada today (China, India, Pakistan and Philippines), although these behaviours and ways of thinking are largely true for the broader Asian population. The broad Asian population includes the six regions:

1. North Asia – Russia (Siberia and the area east of the Ural Mountains)

2. East Asia – Japan, People's Republic of **China**, North Korea, South Korea, Mongolia

3. South Asia **– India, Pakistan**, Bangladesh, Sri Lanka, Nepal, Bhutan, Maldives

4. Southeast Asia – Indonesia, Malaysia, **Philippines,** Singapore, Brunei, Timor-Leste, Burma, Thailand, Laos, Cambodia, Vietnam

5. West Asia (Middle East) – Saudi Arabia, Oman, Jordan, Qatar, Kuwait, United Arab Emirates, Bahrain, Armenia, Azerbaijan, Georgia, Yemen, Iraq, Iran, Afghanistan, Israel, Lebanon, Palestine, Turkey, Cyprus, Syria

6. Central Asia – Kazakhstan, Tajikistan, Kyrgyzstan, Uzbekistan, Turkmenistan

The beginning section of this book explores how we think and the key ways western and eastern societies see the world differently.

The next section explores Canada's immigration roots and the challenges and success Canada has had with immigration from these specific countries historically. This is followed by a section on the different religions embraced by the four nations.

The fourth section explores how Asian immigrants apply for careers in Canada and the disconnect that occurs between their expectations and those of their Canadian employers, specifically in the areas of resume structure and interview strategies.

The fifth and longest section looks at how immigrants from these four societies are dissimilar to employees in western business culture in the way they share information, give feedback, delegate, make decisions and manage conflict and schedules.

The final section addresses issues around language and accents.

Once we unbundle the cultural blueprints of behaviour of our subordinates, colleagues, and ourselves - we can move from immigration to effective workplace integration.

2
INTRODUCTION

Each summer, a tour group of approximately 75 international high school students travel across Canada. They are Rotary Exchange Students and represent over 40 different countries from Australia to South Africa. As a Rotarian, I was involved for several years with hosting the group for the one evening they were in Regina, Saskatchewan, my resident city. During one of these tours, I asked a girl from Denmark if she experienced conflict while spending time with people from so many different cultures in the restrictive and controlled environment of a bus tour. "Absolutely," she said. "When it happens, we just throw up our hands and say, "It's cultural!"

Jeanne Martinson

Wouldn't it be great if the workplace could be like that? When someone communicated in a way that we found odd or wrong (according to our perspective of how good communicators and leaders behave), we could just throw up our hands, acknowledge cultural difference and work towards a mutual understanding?

Unfortunately, when cultures clash, we are more likely to ascribe the source of the other person's behaviour to be something totally different – a defect in their personality or a lack of ability to be a good 'fit' in our team or organization.

Cultural differences often lead to conflict which, if not interpreted correctly, can lead to a downward spiral where we minimize the skills of the other person and underestimate the value of their contribution to the organization.

If we have cultural awareness, however, we can understand why another person thinks and behaves differently than we do. Then we can work towards mutual understanding with a goal of increased workplace efficiency and productivity.

3
HOW WE THINK

John, Diana and Sophia are in a meeting where they are discussing a recent conference that they organized for the visiting engineers from their company's plants in India and Mexico. The event went well overall but there were problems in both scheduling of transportation and simultaneous translation services.

Diana leaned on the board table and pointed at John,
"Well THAT was a total disaster. Your people really underperformed, John."
Sophia, squirmed in her seat and said,
"Well Diana, why don't we start with what went well."
Diana sat back in her chair and responded,
"I am sure John wants to know how his team failed. How else can they improve?"

What happened here? Are you thinking Diana is quite a shrew? Would you be uncomfortable, squirming in your seat like Sophia? If you are John, are you shocked? Appreciative? Annoyed?

What are you thinking as you witness this scene where Diane is giving John negative feedback on his team's performance?

When we experience life - a conversation in which we are engaged, a scene we witness, a song we hear on the radio - we take in information about the experience through our five senses (visual, auditory, kinesthetic, olfactory and gustatory). This information is filtered by our mind as we delete information, focus in on other data, distort the information according to our beliefs and values, and generalize so it makes sense to us. It is further affected by our own intention or motivation if we had the same behaviour.

B (Behaviour)
+
I (Intention)
+
I (Interpretation)
=
T (Truth or reality)

Behaviour observed plus our **intention** or motivation if we had the same behaviour plus our **interpretation** of the situation based on our values, beliefs and how we focus, delete, distort and generalize equals what we think is **truth** or the reality of the situation.

When taking in information, very few people stop to ask themselves, "I wonder what that meant?" We usually instantly react, without realizing that our reaction is based on our mental programming and that we are functioning in a habitual, unconscious way.

We delete or discount information that does not agree with our current belief system – we focus in on information that agrees with our beliefs.

Like a front door with a screen insert to let in fresh air, when the information blowing through builds and strengthens our belief, our mind lets it in. When the data disagrees with a belief we hold, we discount, delete, disagree or disbelieve its validity - basically slamming the screen shut.

I once worked with a First Nations woman who was both a successful entrepreneur and a great inspiration to others. When describing the entrepreneur's success to a colleague of mine, my colleague found it hard to believe that this woman was both successful and First Nations. With every new piece of evidence I put in front of her, she disagreed or suggested my information must be incorrect. At the end of our discussion, she amended her judgment to suggest that if this woman was actually successful, then it was "probably because she was raised in a white home and was able to rise above her heritage." Her unyielding stance clearly demonstrated that beliefs that we hold about others different than ourselves can be so powerful that we are unable to absorb evidence that disagrees with that belief. .

My mother is an unrelenting Toronto Blue Jays baseball fan. If I point out a recent loss, challenging her belief that they are the greatest team on the planet, she finds a reason or excuse to defend her belief. It might be that the team currently is having coaching issues or struggling with a tight playing schedule that is causing lack of sleep and poor performance. Even the weather under the covered Toronto Sky Dome has been used for justification.

The point of these two examples is that we will go to great effort to defend the beliefs we hold. We will use excuses, arguments, alternative data, even violence. It takes a self-reflective person to say to herself or himself, "That doesn't agree with what I know or believe. Could I be wrong? Should I investigate further?"

When we are shown evidence that **supports** our belief, we accept that information like a cool breeze drifting through the screen on the door. We respond to ourselves or others by saying, "See, just as I expected."

We constantly have our beliefs reaffirmed by our own selective focus. When the Blue Jays win, my mother's belief in their superiority is reinforced. When my colleague reads about an Indigenous person whose life is troubled, her belief in caucasian superiority is reinforced.

As we age, without questioning ourselves about what we focus on, we become more of who we already are and our beliefs are further cemented.

Our minds are fluid and we distort information.

In a moment, I am going to ask you not to think.
Do not think of a tree with a huge trunk with rough brown bark.
And whatever you do, do not put shiny green leaves on the tree or juicy red apples.
Especially not the kind of apple that crunches when you bite into it.
Don't think about trees.
Don't think about shiny green leaves that rustle in the breeze.
Don't think about apples.

When I use these instructions in an exercise in my diversity workshops, the rare person has the ability to see the tree and quickly change it, or block the tree by sheer will. Most people are more visual and try hard to block the image but are more susceptible to the suggestion of the tree I drew with words.

We visualize what we hear. We see in pictures. Even though I said, "don't", people still saw the tree. In the workshop, if I then ask the participants to see oranges in the tree instead of apples, they can easily picture the tree with oranges in their mind's eye. They have changed their perspective of the truth in an instant.

Because our mind sees in pictures, when conflict happens in the workplace, the more quickly it is resolved the less chance there will be for the parties involved to unconsciously take editorial license with the incident's facts. There will be less time for colleagues to ask questions and suggest, "Are you sure it was apples? It might have been oranges."

Memory expert and socio-linguist, Elizabeth Loftus suggests, *"Memories don't just fade ... they grow. What fades is the initial perception, the actual experience of the events. But every time we recall an event, we must reconstruct the memory, and with each recollection the memory may be changed— colored by succeeding events, other people's recollections or suggestions. Truth and reality, when seen through the filter of our memories, are not objective facts, but subjective, interpretative realities."* (1)

The ability to distort is real and profound. Our mind is fluid, easily changed and rarely flawless.

To learn about our world, we create generalizations.

Our beliefs come from various sources. We inherit them from our parents, learn them from our teachers, accept them from our religious leaders, and adopt them from our celebrity idols.

We often follow the same political and religious beliefs of our parents until the challenging years of adolescence. We learn beliefs from our teachers through curriculm design, lecture content and consequences for good and bad behaviours. We absorb beliefs through media - whether we are a newspaper reading Baby Boomer or a Gen Y Snapchatter.

A further source of beliefs are generalizations. This is when we have one or few experiences with something and generalize this to be true for everything of that category. This is a key ingredient in our ability to learn, but this same unconscious skill can create inaccurate beliefs when applied to people instead of things.

Most of us have had the experience of driving a car with the gearshift on the steering column. When attempting to drive a vehicle with the gearshift on the console for the first time, how did we know that the gearshift had the same purpose? Chances are that those handy letters D, R, P were also present. Car A is similar to Car B. A puts the car in gear. Perhaps B does as well.

Doorknobs are usually round and located half way up the door.

If we turn the knob and push or pull, the door opens. If after years of round doorknob experiences, what if we were to come across a rectangular doorknob? How would we know what to do? A is similar to B. A opens the door. Maybe B does as well.

Generalizations can create beliefs about groups of people.

Unfortunately, what works well with doorknobs does not necessarily work well with people. If we have an experience with a person from a particular country or religious group, and we allow our mind to make that experience represent the entire group, we are in danger of generalizing to the point of stereotyping.

Although some may argue that this may give us some information 'in a general way' as to issues, needs or behaviours of a group, the danger of negating individuality for the sake of this argument is risky. The research, to be covered in a later chapter, describing how we identify easterners and westerners as relationship-focused and individual-focused respectively, is based on data involving thousands of people and many studies. It is important to look at trends, without falling for absolutes.

An expression in media is 'if it bleeds, it leads'. No news is no news and good news is no news. Death, murder, and scandal are what hit the news and many people who have no experience with people from certain groups may make judgments based on media alone. These judgments then become the beliefs from which we see members of that particular group.

For some of us, our only exposure to people who are different from ourselves comes through the safe cultural lens of on-line media, a movie screen, music CD, book cover, or an evening newscast. This distance from personal connection can create a mono-cultural perspective where we embrace broad stereotypes to identify cultural difference and accept simplistic perceptions of cultural difference and commonality.

If we get our information from media alone and do not monitor our ability to unconsciously generalize, it is a quick two-step dance to beliefs and negative stereotypes.

4
EASTERN WESTERN THINKING

Easterners (such as East Indians and Filipinos) and westerners (such as Canadians, Americans and Europeans) perceive the world and approach it in very different ways. When managing across cultures, the most significant difference for managers to consider is the macro/relationship focus of easterners and the micro/individual focus of westerners.

In the address below, for example, easterners begin with the big picture (Canada) and narrow it down to the first name of the person living in the home. Westerners begin with the specific and move up to the macro or holistic picture. (That is why many Asian names have the surname first, not second.)

Western thought:
Jeff Trueheart

2885 Colander Road
Anytown, Ontario, Canada

(Jeff Tibo lives at 2885 Colander Road in the city of Anytown, in the Province of Ontario, in the country of Canada)

Eastern Thought:
Canada
Anytown
2885 Colander Road
Trueheart Jeff

(In the country of Canada, in the Province of Ontario, in the city of Anytown, on the road named Colander, in the house with the number 2885, lives a man with the surname Tibo and the first name Jeff).

Westerners generally see space as something that is mostly empty. It is the thing in which planets float. Objects in empty space exist independently of their surroundings. But to easterners (particularly citizens of China, Korea and Japan), space has been believed since ancient times to be filled with energy connecting all objects.

This connection to all things can be seen in the way that easterners see relationships to not only objects but to people.

In an experiment by researchers Takahiko Masuda and Richard E. Nisbett, westerners (Americans) and easterners (Japanese) were asked to look at two pictures and answer the question: Is the central character (the man at the front wearing the shirt with the number 2 on the front) happy?

Picture A

Picture B

The findings: the Americans generally said that the main character was happy, both in picture A and picture B. The Japanese participants described the main character as happy in picture A, but not in picture B.

One of the researchers, Professor of Psychology at University of Alberta, Takahiko Masuda, believes that "North Americans in general are likely to focus only on the center of the scene - the central character. Even though the background has been changed from one group of smiling people to a group of frowning people, North American viewers do not care or notice. They focus on the central character. It was as if the people in the background did not exist (picture C).

Picture C

The Japanese, however, are strongly influenced by the changes in the facial expressions of the people in the background. If you are presented with a happy background, the happy central character is seen as much happier than in the case where they are presented with a sad or neutral background.

In another experiment, the same researchers studied the eye movements of easterners and westerners as they viewed a video of a tiger in the jungle. The Americans focused in on the most salient object and spent nearly all the time looking at the tiger. Asians spent much more time looking at the background and especially looking back and forth between the background and the object - back and forth between the jungle and the tiger. In eastern thought, the property of an object can differ depending on where it is. So a tiger in a zoo or a circus is perceived differently from one in the jungle. Easterners over-analyze the situation or environment of an object compared to westerners. Westerners do not have a systemic focus beyond the central character.

Traditional portraits in the east have broad backgrounds and typical portraits in the west have smaller perspectives and focus in tightly on central objects. To see if these differences could be spotted in modern society, the researchers performed a third study. They asked college students from eastern and western countries to take pictures of their friends. Western students mostly took large pictures of faces with a small background. Eastern students balanced the space in the photo between the people and the background.

In a fourth study, the researchers used a picture of three things: a monkey, a panda bear and a bunch of bananas. Easterners and westerners were asked to identify which two of the three items belong together. Westerners *categorized* the objects, stating that the two things that belonged together were the monkey and panda bear as they were both animals and mammals. They noticed how the panda bear and monkey were of the same categories in several ways.

Easterners said the two things that belonged together were the monkeys and the bananas as there was a *relationship* between the monkey and the bananas – the monkey eats the bananas.

When westerners see objects, they separate them from their background and interpret their meaning. They are inclined to attend to a specific focal object, analyzing its attributes and categorizing it in an effort to find out what rules govern its behavior. To find the answer to why the object or person behaves the way it does, the questioner focuses exclusively on the object.

Easterners, however, are more likely to attend to a broad perceptual and conceptual field, noticing relationships and changes, and grouping objects based on relationship rather than category membership. Why an object or person behaves the way it does is connected to the context or environment in which it exists.

People as individuals versus part of a group

The western-style independent and largely unconnected self is difficult for easterners to comprehend. Asian philosopher, H. Shih in his book, *An Outline of the History of Chinese Philosophy*, reminds easterners that, "Man cannot exist alone - all action must be in the form of interaction between man and man."

East Asians live in complex social networks with prescribed role relations. Attention to context is important to effective functioning.

Westerners, however, live in less constraining social worlds and have the luxury of focusing on one object or person and their personal goals regarding that object or person.

Anthropologist Edward T. Hall, in his book, *Beyond Culture*, introduced the concept of "low context" versus "high context" societies to capture this difference in social relations. The western self is composed of fixed attributes and can move from one setting or context to another without significant alteration (therefore low context). But for East Asians, the person is so connected to others that the self is literally dependent on the context (therefore high context). As philosopher Donald Munro put it, East Asians understand themselves in terms of their relation to the whole, such as the family and society. If an important person is removed from the individual's social network, that individual literally becomes a different person.

Self-descriptions capture these differences. When asked to describe themselves, Americans and Canadians describe more of their personality traits and attitudes than do Japanese. North Americans tend to focus on their distinctiveness and to prefer uniqueness in themselves and in their possessions. In one study done by researcher H. Kim and H.R. Markus, Koreans and Americans were given a choice among different colored pens to have as a gift. Americans chose the rarest colour, whereas Koreans chose the most common colour.

Societal training for independence versus interdependence begins early. Where it is common for western babies to sleep in a different bed from their parents (or even in a different room), this is rare for Asian babies. Adults from several generations often surround the Chinese baby.

Even in play, researchers A. Fernald and H. Morikawa found there is a difference in how objects and people are described to children. When American mothers play with their children, they tend to focus their attention on objects and their attributes such as "see the truck; it has nice wheels". Japanese mothers emphasize feelings and relationships, not categorizing or drawing attention to the parts or uniqueness of the object. They might say things such as "when you throw your truck, the wall says, 'ouch'".

For the past several years, the majority of new Canadians have been arriving from the eastern countries of China, Philippines, Pakistan and India. Managers and leaders who grasp the marked difference between eastern and western thought and how these mindsets affect the workplace will be more effective at recruiting, retaining and engaging their diverse workforce.

5
CANADA'S IMMIGRANT ROOTS

The continuous flow of foreigners coming to its shores has been integral to Canada's success. In the beginning, this movement of humanity was not driven by immigration to develop a new land. It was propelled by a desire for resources, a claim for sovereignty for home nations, and just dumb luck.

"Welcome to Barneyland!" That might be what we would say instead of "Welcome to Canada!" if only Barney had come ashore.

A Viking saga tells of an island trader named Bjarni (Barney) Herjolfsson, around 985 CE who returned home from Europe to find his father had left for a new settlement on Greenland. Barney set off west to follow and was blown off course in the fog. He landed in a new country dense with trees and covered with small hills.

Barney did not go ashore. He realized his navigational error, turned his boat around and set off for home. He did, however, tell the tale of his misadventure. Perhaps it started, "You think you've made a wrong turn!"[1]

Leif Ericson (the son of Eric the Red who founded the Greenland colony) believed Barney's tall tale, bought the misadventurer's boat and sailed off in a southwesterly direction from Greenland. When Ericson landed, he called the place Vinland (which means land of grapes, or berries, or meadows - depending who you ask). This first documented contact in 1000 CE was between the Norse and either the Dorset or Beothuk natives in Labrador.[2]

The Vikings' brief and gloomy stay is recorded in Norse myth and Canadian history. They built sod houses on the coast and repaired their ships using local iron deposits. Other Vikings made the trip to the tiny settlement as well, but eventually the Vikings abandoned the settlement.[3]

What if Portugal had taken more decisive action over their awarded territories? We might be speaking Portuguese as our official language today.

In 1493, Pope Alexander VI established a line between Spanish and Portuguese territory in present day Canada. According to his declaration (also known as a Papal Bull), the lands to the west of this line were to be a Spanish monopoly and lands east, including Newfoundland and present day Nova Scotia, were to be Portuguese territory. This was further strengthened with a Spanish – Portuguese treaty, the Treaty of Tordesillas, a year later. [4]

In 1501 and 1502, the Portuguese brothers Gaspar and Miguel Corte Real mapped an extensive portion of the North American seaboard. European cartographers felt free to name what lands they encountered and evidence of the Portuguese endeavors dot maps of Canada today with names such as the Bay of Fundy (Portuguese for deep bay) and Labrador (Lavrador meaning farmer).

But the Papal Bull of 1493 was to divide the land between Spain and Portugal and the English and French felt they had no duty to uphold an agreement they were not party to. When Cabot arrived in 1497, in what was clearly Portuguese territory, he followed the Charter from England's Henry VII. It specified that he could not enter lands already discovered by the Portuguese, he interpreted to mean that unless there was obvious previous occupation, England was welcome to the territory.

Around 1521, a few dozen Portuguese families landed on the shores of the new world. They were armed with a charter from King Manuel of Portugal to establish a colony that could serve as a base for industry and trade. The settlers represented a last desperate attempt by the Portuguese to assert their claim to North America. Their colony predates the settlement of Port-Royal, which is considered to be Canada's first permanent European settlement, by more than 80 years. Unfortunately, the colony disappeared and no one knows what became of Portugal's last ditch attempt.

The prolific fishing off Newfoundland kept several European countries hovering about the shores of Canada. However, the desire for further resources eventually drove the French and English into more permanent relationships with the land and the Indigenous people who lived there.

As Europeans began settling in Canada, so too began our love/hate relationship with immigration. Who should come in? From where? Where should they settle? What kinds of jobs do we need them to do? How will it affect those who already live here? Who should get rights? Who should control the economic, religious and political power of the new land?

There have been three distinctive and significant waves of immigration to Canada in the past 500 years.

The initial wave was of farmer settlers, missionaries and fur traders, primarily from France, England and Scotland.

The second wave, beginning around 1870, consisted mainly of immigrants from Europe to settle western Canada and build eastern Canadian infrastructure and industry. In this same time period, immigrants were also sought from China, primarily to build the trans-continental railroad.

In our third and current wave of immigration, immigrants are sought based on a point system, not on country of origin. New immigrants are more likely to be from non-European countries and to be non-Caucasian.

On the chart following, note that data from the 2011 census sets Canada's population at 32,852,320 people – of which 6,775,765 are immigrants. This means Canada's foreign-born population is 20.6% of the total population - the highest proportion among the G8 countries.

91% of immigrants who have arrived in the 2005-2011 time frame speak English or French and 93.5% of immigrants overall speak English or French.

Between 2006 and 2011, approximately 1,162,900 foreign-born people immigrated to Canada. These recent immigrants make up 17.2% of the foreign-born population and 3.5% of the total population in Canada. Asia is Canada's largest source of immigrants during this five year span, although the share of immigration from Africa, Caribbean, Central and South America increased slightly.

The five top source countries where immigrants are coming to Canada from today are Philippines, India, China, Iran and Pakistan. (In late 2016 to early 2017, Canada accepted more than 30,000 refugees from Syria. It is unpredictable as to whether this immigration from Syria will continue to be a long term trend.).

Between 2006 and 2011, about 145,700 immigrants arrived from Africa which represents 12.5% of the newcomers who arrived during that five year span. This is up from 10.3% among those who arrived during the previous five-year period. In contrast, individuals born in Africa accounted for 7.3 % of immigrants during the 1990s and 1.9% of immigrants who arrived in Canada prior to 1971.

Number of Languages Spoken (2011)

	Total Population		Non-immigrants		Immigrants		Recent Immigrants (2006 to 2011)	
	number	percentage	number	percentage	number	percentage	number	percentage
Total population	32,852,320	100.0	25,720,170	100.0	5,775,765	100.0	1,162,915	100.0
Speaks one language	20,819,655	63.4	19,014,880	73.9	1,725,700	25.5	226,210	19.5
English only	16,542,730	50.4	15,208,855	59.1	1,278,505	18.9	116,450	10.0
French only	3,774,750	11.5	3,709,135	14.4	59,865	0.9	17,995	1.5
Non-official language only	502,175	1.5	96,890	0.4	387,330	5.7	91,765	7.9
Speaks more than one language	12,032,665	36.6	6,705,290	26.1	5,050,055	74.5	936,695	80.5
Both official languages only	4,369,345	13.3	4,178,205	16.2	176,830	2.6	24,965	2.1
Both official languages and one or more non-official languages	1,402,910	4.3	699,455	2.7	673,305	9.9	121,680	10.5
One official language and one or more non-official languages	6,206,660	18.9	1,826,150	7.1	4,149,060	61.2	776,975	66.8
Multiple non-official languages only	53,750	0.2	1,480	0.0	50,860	0.8	13,075	1.1

New Permanent Residents By Country Year: 2015 (Canada)

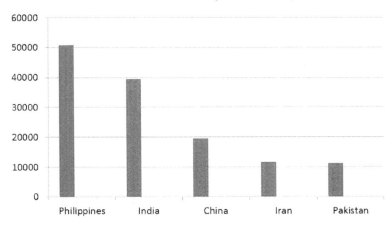

People born in the Caribbean, Central and South America represented 12.3% of all newcomers between 2006 and 2011, up from 10.5% from those who came during the five years earlier.

The share of recent immigrants from the United States increased slightly to 3.9% from 3.2% during the years 2001 to 2005.

So clearly, immigration is not new to Canada. Immigration has created consistent population growth and economic success for Canada.

6
THE INDIA-PAKISTAN DIVORCE

In August of 1947, after three hundred years in India, the British finally left. The subcontinent was partitioned into two independent nation states: Hindu-majority India and Muslim-majority Pakistan. Immediately, there began one of the greatest migrations in human history, as millions of Muslims trekked to West and East Pakistan (the latter now known as Bangladesh) while millions of Hindus and Sikhs headed in the opposite direction. Many hundreds of thousands never made it.

Across the Indian subcontinent, communities that had coexisted for almost a thousand years attacked each other in a terrifying outbreak of sectarian violence, with Hindus and Sikhs on one side and Muslims on the other - a mutual genocide as unexpected as it was unprecedented. By 1948, as the great migration drew to a close, more than fifteen million people had been uprooted, and between one and two million were dead.

This 'Partition' of India into two countries is central to modern identity in the Indian subcontinent. Memories of almost unimaginable violence is branded painfully into the consciousness of its citizens. Pakistani historian, Ayesha Jalal called Partition, "the central historical event in twentieth century South Asia. It was a defining moment that is neither beginning nor end, partition continues to influence how the peoples and states of postcolonial South Asia envisage their past, present and future."

How did this unified society turn on itself?

After WWII, Britain simply no longer had the resources with which to control its greatest imperial asset and its exit from India was messy and hasty. From the vantage point of the retreating colonizers, it was unexpectedly successful. Whereas British rule in India had long been marked by violent revolts and brutal suppressions, the British Army was able to march out of the country with barely a shot fired and only seven casualties.

Equally unexpected was the ferocity of the ensuing bloodbath.

Until the middle of the 20th century, India had a deeply intermixed and surprisingly unified culture (in spite of possessing the three religions of Islam, Hinduism and Sikhism).

The first Islamic conquests of India happened with the capture of Lahore in 1021. Although the conquests themselves were marked by carnage and by the destruction of Hindu and Buddhist sites, India soon embraced and transformed the new arrivals. Within a few centuries, a hybrid Indo-Islamic civilization emerged, along with hybrid languages which mixed the Sanskrit-based vernaculars of India with Turkish, Persian, and Arabic words.

Eventually, around a fifth of South Asia's population came to identify as Muslim. The Sufi mystics associated with the spread of Islam often regarded the Hindu scriptures as divinely inspired. In village folk traditions, the practice of the two faiths came close to blending into one. Hindus would visit the graves of Sufi masters and

Muslims would leave offerings at Hindu shrines.

In the 17th century, the Mughal crown prince Dara Shikoh had a study of Hinduism and Islam created and "The Mingling of Two Oceans" stressed the affinities of the two faiths. The last Mughal emperor, enthroned in 1837, wrote that Hinduism and Islam "share the same essence," and his court lived out this ideal at every level.

In the 19th century, India was still a place where traditions, languages, and cultures cut across religious groupings, and where people did not define themselves primarily through their religious faith. A Sunni Muslim weaver from Bengal, for example, would have had far more in common in his language, outlook, and his fondness for fish with one of his Hindu colleagues than he would with a Shia Muslim from Karachi who lived in the North-West Frontier.

Many writers blame the British for the gradual erosion of these shared traditions. When the British started to define communities based on religious identity and attach political representation to them, many Indians stopped accepting the diversity of their own thoughts and began to ask themselves in which of the boxes they belonged. From the earlier chapter on eastern and western thought, you can now see how the western idea of categorization over the eastern idea of relationship to upset the equilibrium of the nation.

Other assessments emphasize that Partition, far from emerging inevitably out of a policy of British divide-and-rule, was largely a development to address a brewing problem. There was a clash of personalities among the politicians of the period, particularly between Muhammad Ali Jinnah (the leader of the Muslim League) and Mohandas Gandhi and Jawaharlal Nehru (the prominent leaders of the Hindu-dominated Congress Party). All three men were lawyers who had received at least part of their education in England.

Jinnah was a surprising creator for the Islamic Republic of Pakistan. He was a secularist, drank whiskey, rarely went to a mosque, was clean-shaven and stylish, and wore Savile Row suits and silk ties. Significantly, he chose to marry a non-Muslim woman who was famous for her beautiful saris.

Jinnah, wanted religion kept out of South Asian politics and resented the way Gandhi brought spiritual sensibilities into the political discussion. In the early part of his political career, Jinnah strove to bring together the Muslim League and the Congress Party and in 1916, he belonged to both parties. He succeeded in getting them to present the British with a common set of demands, the Lucknow Pact, and was hailed as the Ambassador of Hindu-Muslim Unity.

Jinnah continued to fight for a secular India, but Gandhi was going in a different direction. In 1920, Jinnah was booed off a Congress Party stage when he insisted on calling his rival "Mr. Gandhi" rather than referring to him by his spiritual title, Mahatma or Great Soul. Throughout the 1920s and 1930s, Gandhi and Jinnah's mutual dislike grew, and by 1940, Jinnah had steered the Muslim League toward demanding a separate homeland for the Muslim minority of South Asia.

Even after his demands for the creation of Pakistan were met, Jinnah insisted that his new country would guarantee freedom of religious expression. In August 1947, in his first address to the Constituent Assembly of Pakistan, he said, "You may belong to any religion, or caste, or creed - that has nothing to do with the business of the State."

But it was too late. By the time the speech was delivered, violence between Hindus and Muslims had spiraled beyond anyone's ability to control it.

Hindus and Muslims had begun to turn on each other during the chaos unleashed by WWII. In 1942, as the Japanese seized Singapore and advanced toward India, the Congress Party began a campaign of civil disobedience and its leaders, including Gandhi and Nehru, were arrested. While they were in prison, Jinnah, who had billed himself as a loyal ally of the British, consolidated opinion behind him as the best protection of Muslim interests against Hindu dominance.

From that point on, violence on the streets between Hindus and Muslims began to escalate. People moved away from, or were forced out of, mixed neighborhoods and took refuge in increasingly polarized ghettos.

Tensions were often heightened by local and regional political leaders. The first series of widespread religious massacres took place in Calcutta in 1946. As riots spread to other cities and the number of casualties escalated, the leaders of the Congress Party, who had initially opposed Partition, began to see it as the only way to rid themselves of the troublesome Jinnah and his Muslim League.

In a speech in April 1947, Nehru said, *"I want that those who stand as an obstacle in our way should go their own way."*

Likewise, the British realized that they had lost any remaining vestiges of control and began to speed up their exit strategy. On the afternoon of February 20, 1947, the British Prime Minister, Clement Atlee, announced that British rule would end on "a date not later than June, 1948." If Nehru and Jinnah could be reconciled by then, power would be transferred to "some form of central Government for British India." If not, they would hand over authority "in such other way as may seem most reasonable and in the best interests of the Indian people."

In March, 1947, a minor royal named Lord Louis Mountbatten flew into Delhi as Britain's final Viceroy, his mission to hand over power and get out of India as quickly as possible. A series of disastrous meetings with Jinnah soon convinced him that the Muslim League leader was impervious to negotiation. Worried that if he didn't move rapidly, Britain might end up refereeing a civil war, Mountbatten deployed his considerable diplomatic skill to persuade all the parties to agree to Partition as the only remaining option.

None of the disputants were happy with the compromise that Mountbatten had forced on them. Jinnah, who had succeeded in creating a new country, regarded the truncated state he was given a sad disappointment and that the partition of Punjab and Bengal would be sowing the seeds of future serious trouble.

On August 14, 1947, Nehru rose to his feet to make his most famous speech. "Long years ago, we made a tryst with destiny," he declaimed. "At the stroke of the midnight hour, when the world sleeps, India will awake to life and freedom."

What followed, especially in Punjab, the principal center of the violence, was one of the great human tragedies of the twentieth century.

Within a few months, the landscape of South Asia had changed irrevocably. In 1941, Karachi (designated the first capital of Pakistan) was 47.6 per cent Hindu and Delhi (the capital of independent India) was one-third Muslim. By the end of the decade, almost all the Hindus of Karachi had fled, while two hundred thousand Muslims had been forced out of Delhi. The changes made in a matter of months remain indelible seventy years later.

Ever since 1947, India and Pakistan have nourished a deep-rooted mutual antipathy. They have fought two inconclusive wars over the disputed region of Kashmir - the only Muslim-majority area to remain within India. In 1971, they fought over the secession of East Pakistan (which became Bangladesh). In 1999, after Pakistani troops crossed into an area of Kashmir called Kargil, the two countries came alarmingly close to a nuclear exchange.

Despite periodic gestures toward peace negotiations, the India-Pakistan conflict rooted in the pain of partition remains the dominant geopolitical reality of the region.

7
FROM INDIA AND PAKISTAN
TO CANADA

In the previous chapter, we examined the history of Pakistan and India. Although they are two very different nations today, these two countries share a common history when it comes to immigration to Canada. Citizens from both nations integrate well into the Canadian workplace, partially due to their shared experience of the influence of Britain on their language and culture.

A Brief History of Indian Immigration

The first visitors to Canada from India were Sikh soldiers in the British Indian Army in 1897. They were travelling on their way from London, England to their home base in Hong Kong where they served the British Empire. They took home tales of the great land of opportunity that was Canada – a nation open to them for immigration as British subjects.

The first documented immigrants from the Indian subcontinent were of the Sikh denomination who arrived in Vancouver in 1904. They found jobs in the industries of agriculture, fishing and forestry.

Although British Columbia was happy to have hard working and cheap labour for industry, they were not willing to give Indian (or Chinese or Japanese) immigrants the right to vote. This restriction limited Asian immigrants from voting federally or working within a profession (such as doctors, lawyers, pharmacists or engineers).

At the time, any British citizen had the right to travel and live in any country of the empire, including Canada. The Canadian government, however, was interested in attracting only Caucasian European immigrants so, in 1908, the government passed two orders-in-council to restrict Indian immigration.

The first order-in-council required that Indian immigrants begin their journey in India and come directly to Canada. This continuous journey from the sub-continent to North America was almost impossible in the time period before air travel. To ensure the law's effectiveness, the government also discouraged all shipping companies from providing direct passage from India to Canada.

The second law required that each immigrant from India possess $200, while only demanding European immigrants to possess $25.

These two laws orders in council effectively stopped Indian immigration. It also meant that Indian immigrants who were already in Canada could not bring their wives or children to the country.

Immigration numbers of these early years reflect these changes. Note the drop in the graph on the next page. From 2623 immigrants in 1907, numbers dropped to a mere three immigrants in 1908.

The Komagata Maru

An Indian businessman, Gurdit Singh, decided to challenge the laws. He chartered a ship in 1914 and sailed from Hong Kong to

India Immigration
Decrease/Increase/Decrease
From 45 in 1904 to 2623 in 1907 to less than 10

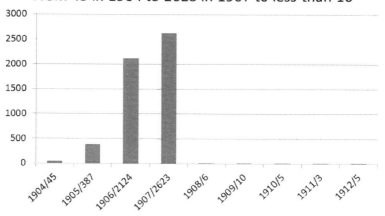

Vancouver with 375 fellow Indians aboard. The *Komagata Maru* arrived in Vancouver on May 23, 1914.

Immigration officers refused to let the passengers get off the boat, which was made to anchor offshore. Canadian authorities refused to provide food and water for the first two weeks after the ship's arrival, creating widespread suffering. The passengers were kept prisoner on the ship for two months with limited food and water while lawyers, politicians and immigration officials argued about their case – with the final outcome being expulsion.

When the passengers arrived back in India, they were met by British police who tried to send them directly to the Punjab region of India (the farthest region from a shipping port). A riot broke out - twenty passengers were killed, many were injured and hundreds were arrested.

Limiting Indian immigration to Canada was a strategic action by the British government as it was worried that a large overseas Indian population might support the rise up against British rule in India. The

Punjabi community (primarily of the Sikh faith), particularly, considered limits to Indian immigration an insult. Sikhs had long been in regiments of the British Indian Army and had remained loyal to the British regime. The lack of British support for immigration was seen as a betrayal.

In 1918, Canadian Prime Minister Robert Borden was pressured by British officials to halt the growing dissent and support for India's independence within the Indian-Canadian community. The Canadian government changed the policy so that Indian immigrants already in Canada could bring their wives and children to Canada.

In 1947, when India achieved independence from Britain, partition split India into two nations – India and Pakistan. In 1967, Canada made sweeping changes to its immigration policy and a new wave of Indian immigrants came to Canada.

In the 1960s, Canada began to transition toward a policy of multiculturalism that eliminated many discriminatory immigration policies. As a direct result, within a few short years, the Indian population in Canada multiplied more than 20 times over. By this time, immigrants from all parts of India and Pakistan, with a wide array of religions, were choosing to migrate to Canada. This upward trajectory of immigration continues today.

In August 2008, Prime Minister Harper publicly apologized for the treatment of the passengers on the ship, the Komagata Mura.

Indian Immigration to Canada Today

Today, approximately 30,000 Indian citizens become new permanent residents of Canada each year. In 2013 alone, 33,000 Indians were issued permanent resident visas. 14,000 students arrived in the country, and a full 130,000 came to Canada as visitors. Many permanent residents were able to sponsor family members and this reunification of families strengthened communities across the country.

Indo-Canadians are the third largest non-European immigrant group in the country, after residents of Chinese and Filipino descent. It is also one of Canada's most prominent and well-integrated communities.

Many new arrivals from India speak business level English and possess experience in key industries like information technology, science, and medicine. These skills, combined with the Indian community's strong support network, means that many newcomers are often able to quickly find jobs and settle into their new homes after arriving in Canada.

8
FROM CHINA TO CANADA

Fifty lone Chinese arrived in 1788 on the western shore of Canada.

British Columbia paid little attention to the influx of Chinese. The new immigrants worked as gold prospectors, then labourers building roads. They found work in domestic and laundry services and other jobs that were at the bottom of the economic ladder.

The second wave of immigrants from China began in 1881 to fill jobs as workers to build the transcontinental railway. 17,000 Chinese workers worked on the four-year project.

However, in 1885, the racial backlash of thousands of mostly male Chinese immigrants was swift and fierce.

As vital as the Chinese were to the building of Canada as a nation, citizens of Canada pushed for legislation to deal with what they considered the 'Yellow Peril' that threatened their way of life.

A head tax was levied in 1885 on all Chinese immigrants, the only racial group to be subject to such an entry fee. The intention was to limit immigration from China. The head tax was increased from $50 to $100 in 1900. It was further raised from $100 to $500 in 1903.

In 1923, the Government of Canada enacted the Chinese Immigration Act (Chinese Exclusion Act) which shut the door on any immigration from China. This left thousands of men stranded in Canada, with wives and children on the other side of the world. The choice – return to family if one had the money for the ship fare – or stay in Canada and support loved ones economically from afar.

When Canada declared war on Japan during WWII, Canada and China had a common enemy – Japan. The victorious end of the war in 1945 marked a milestone in Chinese-Canadian history. The attitude of Canadians shifted and in 1947, the Chinese Immigration Act was repealed and the right to vote was granted. By 1967, all anti-Chinese clauses were removed from Canada's immigration laws.

In 2006, Prime Minister Stephen Harper formally apologized on behalf of the Government of Canada for the discriminatory policies of the past related to the head tax and exclusion act. The handful of head tax payers still alive were compensated for the money they lost at that time.

Chinese Immigration Today

Since 1947, Canada has welcomed Chinese immigrants with open arms. In fact, today China is the second largest source country for new immigrants. Between 2006 and 2011, over 122,000 Chinese nationals became permanent residents in Canada. This is 10% of the total immigration to Canada during this five year time period.

Individuals with Chinese ancestry can be found in every Canadian province. There is a particularly strong Chinese presence in Toronto and Vancouver, where 40 per cent and 31 per cent of the country's Chinese residents live respectively.

As perhaps Canada's oldest non-European immigrant community, the Chinese have faced a bumpy road to full integration in Canadian culture. Today, they are the country's largest non-Caucasian ethnic group, numbering over 1,300,000 residents. As thousands of new arrivals come from China each year, both countries are able to benefit from a rich exchange of language, culture, and ideas.

9
FROM PHILIPPINES TO CANADA

Filipino immigration to Canada began late compared to other nations. Only small numbers were recorded in the year 1930. By the 1950s and 1960s, approximately 800 had settled in Canada, almost entirely in Winnipeg, Manitoba. Since the 1990s, immigration from the Philippines had increased steadily, moving to other major centers.

Over the past 25 years, the Filipino community in Canada has gone from fewer than 1000 immigrants, mostly settled in the Winnipeg, Manitoba area, to half a million spread across the nation.

In 2011, 454,340 immigrants listed the Philippines as their place of birth, of which 292,505 had Canadian citizenship. Another 46,615 were listed as non-permanent residents (students and people in the temporary foreign worker programs).

Most people living in Canada who were born in the Philippines live in Ontario (218,660) with the majority in Toronto (185,085), but as a percentage of provincial population, Manitoba has a higher Filipinos population than Ontario.

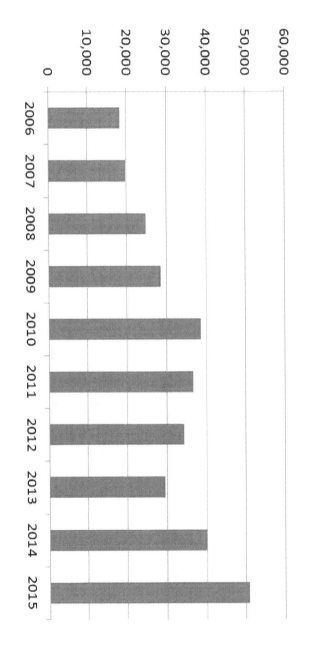

321,742 New Permanent Residents from Philippines landed in Canada (2006-2015)

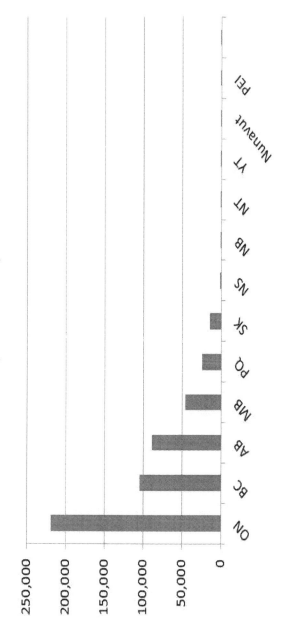

Born in Philippines and Living in Canada

(as of 2011)

Winnipeg has remained a major destination for newcomers from the Philippines, with 10% of all Filipino immigrants living in this city. Now recognized as Winnipeg's largest ethnic minority, Filipinos make up 9% of the city's total population.

The immigration pattern for many Filipinos is first an individual will come to Canada as a temporary worker, leaving spouses and children behind. Once permanent residency is achieved, they are then able to reunite with their families in Canada.

Filipinos in Canada work in a wide range of disciplines in every province in the country. Because many Filipinos have a good command of the English language, they are able to find jobs and quickly settle into their new homes upon arrival.

Many Filipino immigrants find work in one of two popular fields: nursing and care giving. Prospective immigrants with experience in these fields are in luck, as Canada has many immigration programs geared towards workers with these skill sets.

Influence of Language, Religion and Law

The Filipino community has become well integrated into the fabric of Canadian society, more so than other eastern countries. This is due to language, religion and European colonization.

In the Philippines, laws and court decisions, with extremely rare exceptions, are written solely in English. English is also used in higher education, religious affairs, print and broadcast media, and business. Most educated Filipinos are bilinguals and speak English as one of their languages.

For highly technical subjects such as nursing, medicine and information technology, English is the preferred medium for textbooks and communication. In everyday media most television shows and films are not dubbed, but are shown in English only.

English is part of the school curriculum from primary school and Filipinos write and speak fluent Philippine English (which has slight differences in diction and pronunciation).

The first recorded visit by Europeans to the Philippines was by Spain in 1521. Spanish colonization began in 1565, creating the first unified political structure known as the Philippines. Spanish colonial rule saw the introduction of Christianity, a code of law and the oldest modern university in Asia. With Spain's defeat in the Spanish-American War in 1898, the Philippines became a colony of the United States.

American rule was not easily accepted and revolution resulted, with the eventual Philippine Declaration of Independence and the establishment of the First Philippine Republic. The Philippine-American War ensued, with extensive damage and death, ultimately resulting in the defeat of the Philippine Republic.

The United States established the Insular Government to rule the Philippines. In 1907, the Philippine National Assembly was created and elections were held. These were the first nationwide elections ever held in the Philippines and were a turning point in the country's history, for the National Assembly marked the commencement of Filipino participation in self-governance and a big leap towards self-determination.

In 1916, the U.S. Federal Government formally promised independence and the Philippine Commonwealth was established in 1935. This began the 10-year process that led to full independence as an independent Philippine Republic in 1946.

Language, culture, religious influences make immigrants from the Philippine easily adaptable to the existing Canadian culture, but they are still primarily influenced by the differences of thinking as described in the eastern-western chapter. These differences need to be taken into consideration in communicating and leading immigrants from this nation.

10
RELIGIONS OF NEW IMMIGRANTS

The four countries that are the major sources of today's Canadian immigrants (India, Pakistan, Philippines, China) have different predominant religions. This chapter will give managers a fundamental knowledge of the five religions prominent in those areas: Catholicism, Islam, Hinduism, Sikhism, and China's unique combination of folk religion.

Although the **Philippines** is officially a secular state, 81% of the population declared themselves as **Catholic** in their 2010 national census – with over 37% attending Mass regularly. Protestant Christians are a much smaller group at 1.8% of the population. Muslims, 5.7% of the population, are primarily Sunni and are the second largest religious group in the country after the unreligious (10%).

Indian and Pakistan, as you read in Chapter Four, split geographically along religious lines at the time of Partition. Today

97.0% of **Pakistanis** are **Muslim**, the majority being Sunni with an estimated 10-25% Shia Muslim.

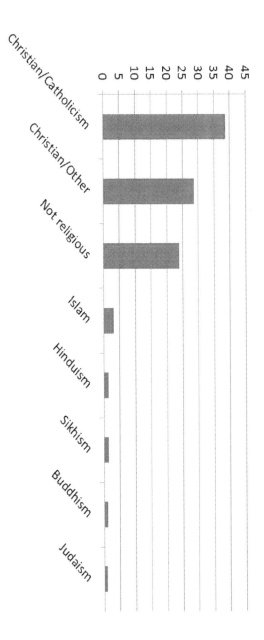

Religious Groups in Canada
by percentage (2011)

After Islam, Hinduism and Christianity are the largest religious groups with 2,800,000 adherents each (1.6% of the population) as of the 2005 census. **Hindus comprise 79.8% of the Indian population.** Muslims represent 14.2% of the population, Sikhs 17% and Christians 2.3%. Proportionately, **Sikhs** from India immigrate in higher numbers to Canada than do Hindus from India.

Chinese civilization has been molded by several religious movements with the three primary influences being the teachings of **Confucius, Buddha and the Tao.** Chinese or 'folk' religion has grown to be a combination of the three and in China today, there is no clear boundary between religions. 80% of the Chinese population declare they practice **Chinese religion** (a form or combination of Chinese folk religions, Taoism, Buddhism and Confucianism) 10-16% declare themselves as Buddhists, 2-4% as Christians, and 1-2% as Muslim.

So how prolific are these faiths in the overall Canadian population?

As you can see by the graph on the previous page, except for Catholicism, these faiths are practiced by only a small percentage of Canadians.

Whether you call it faith or religion, we all believe in something. One who claims to be a skeptic of one set of beliefs is actually a true believer of another set of beliefs.

.

11
CATHOLICISM

Christians are followers of Jesus Christ, a preacher and a teacher who lived over 2,000 years ago in what is today Israel/Palestine. Jesus was born and raised a Jew and gained supporters among ordinary Jews by performing miracles and teaching forgiveness, but the Jewish authorities disapproved and plotted his downfall.

Christians believe that in the last week of his life, Jesus went to Jerusalem for the Jewish feast of Passover. He was arrested while praying in the Garden of Gethsemane and charged with blasphemy. He was nailed to a cross to die. Three days after his death, his disciples found his tomb empty. Christians believe that Jesus rose from the dead and over the following 40 days, Jesus appeared to his disciples several times before ascending to heaven.

The Holy Scriptures of Christianity are found in the *Bible* (a collection of books comprised of the *Old Testament* which also contain the Jewish scriptures of the *Torah* and the New Testament which was written by Christians in the years after Jesus' death). The *New Testament* contains four accounts of Jesus' teaching and life known as the Gospels as well as acts of his disciples. Christians believe the Christian Bible reveals not only God's will but also how Christians should live their lives.

In the centuries following Jesus Christ's death, his disciples spread this message: Jesus was the Christ, or anointed one. Although he lived a human life, he was the Son of God or God in human form. By giving up his own life (as Christians believe Jesus Christ could have avoided his death by crucifixion), he paid the price for human sin. In being born, living, dying by crucifixion and rising from the dead, Jesus gave people the opportunity to know God and to experience God's love and forgiveness.

Christians believe in one God, but refer to three aspects of God - God the Father (creator of everything), God the Son (Jesus) and God the Holy Spirit (God's presence in the world and in our lives). This is known as the Holy Trinity.

Christian special events are celebrations of the events of Jesus' life: Communion (recalls the last supper where Jesus asked his disciples to remember him), Christmas (when Christ was born), Epiphany (visit of three wise men to the infant Jesus), Lent (40 days before Easter when Christians remember their sins to commemorate the 40 days and nights Jesus spent fasting and praying in the desert), Holy week (the week before Easter), Good Friday (the day Jesus died), Easter Sunday (to celebrate Jesus rising from the dead), Feast of the Ascension (Thursday 40 days after Easter Sunday the day on which Jesus ascended into heaven), Pentecost (celebration of God sending down the Holy Spirit to Jesus' disciples whereby they could speak in different languages so that they could spread the good news of Christ).

Sunday is the worship day for Christians, as this was the day they believe that Jesus rose from the dead.

Most Christians share the same basic beliefs, but there are many ways of expressing them. The three main groups are: **Orthodox, Roman Catholic** and **Protestant**. What separated Christians into these main groups were disagreements over authority (who is the true church with the exclusive right and ability to interpret the word of God), and salvation (how a person finds justification from his or her sins).

Roman Catholics represent the largest Christian community with close to 1 billion members worldwide, and 13 million in Canada. According to the doctrine of the Catholic Church, Jesus named his apostle, Peter, as the spiritual leader with cardinals and bishops as the administrative arm guiding and ministering in various geographical locations around the world.

Catholics believe that scripture and 'sacred tradition' are equal in authority and that the teaching authority of the Roman Church has been entrusted to interpret the *Bible* in order to provide one common belief for all. In regards to salvation, Catholics believe that salvation is secured by two things: faith in Christ as their savior and good works.

There are 13 independent and self-governing church **Orthodoxies** with 500,000 practitioners in Canada. This collection of independent orthodoxies began with the split between the Orthodox Patriarch of Constantinople and the Bishop of Rome (the Pope) in 1054. For Orthodox Christians, each region of the map should have its own head or patriarch and that patriarch should control what happens under his jurisdiction and not be subjected to a higher church authority.

From the beginning, there were four Patriarchates: Constantinople, Alexandria, Antioch and Jerusalem. Eleven others were added: Russia, Romania, Serbia, Greece, Georgia, Bulgaria, Cyprus, Czechoslovakia, Poland, Albania and Sinai. Each of these church bodies is independent of each other. Each is governed by a bishop and have equal weight to the other, even though much of orthodox tradition and teaching has been shaped by the first four.

There are many groups of **Protestant** Christians (such as Baptists, Lutherans, Methodists, Episcopalians, Presbyterians, United Church of Christ, Quakers, Mennonites, and Pentecostals) but there are some common elements in the question of authority and salvation. Protestants generally believe in *sola scriptura* and *sola fide*. Sola scriptura means the *Bible* alone is all that is needed for spiritual authority and all the things a Christian needs to know, believe and practice are clearly stated in the scriptures (which are given by inspiration of God). Sola fide means faith alone is the source of salvation. Faith yields good works and salvation (Protestant perspective) versus good works and faith yielding salvation (Catholic perspective).

12
ISLAM

Islam began 1400 years ago in the city of Mecca in western Arabia (now Saudi Arabia) when the prophet Muhammad began proclaiming the message. That message was "there is only one God". Muslims, the followers of Muhammad, believe that Muhammad was the last in a series of prophets through which Allah (God) revealed his wishes for the world. The previous prophets include Moses, Noah and Jesus.

The word Islam comes from the word *submission'* in Arabic and Muslims are people who submit to Allah's will and try to live in a way that is pleasing to Allah.

The Holy book of Muslims is the *Qur'an* (Quran or Koran) and is believed to contain the perfect word of Allah as revealed to Muhammad through the angel Gabriel. The *Qur'an* tells Muslims how to worship, how to treat other people, what to eat and wear, and how to live a good life. Muslims believe that the *Qur'an* has always existed in heaven, written in Arabic on a tablet of stone.

The five central beliefs of Islam are called the Five Pillars of Islam and are:

1. Shahada (the first pillar) is a statement of faith: "There is no God but Allah and Muhammad is his prophet" or "There is no God but Allah and Muhammad is his messenger."

2. Salat (the second pillar) is prayer. The obligatory prayers are said five times a day and are considered a direct link between the worshipper and God. There is no hierarchical authority in Islam, and no priests*, so the prayers are led by a learned person who knows the *Qur'an* and is chosen by the congregation.

The five prayers contain verses from the *Qur'an* and are said in Arabic. Prayers are said at dawn, noon, mid-afternoon, sunset and nightfall. Muslims can pray anywhere. Chapter (Sura) One of the *Koran* is the prayer that is used five times a day in the life of a Muslim. It reads:

"In the name of God
The Compassionate
The Merciful
Praise be to God, Lord of the Universe,
The Compassionate, the Merciful,
Sovereign of the Day of Judgment!
You alone we worship,
and to You alone we turn for help
Guide us to the straight path
The path of those whom you have favoured,
Not of those who have incurred Your wrath,
Nor of those who have gone astray."

3. Zakat (the third pillar) is the giving of alms to the poor and needy. All things belong to God, and wealth is, therefore, held in trust by

humans. Zakat means growth and purification. Our possessions are purified by setting aside a portion for those in need.

4. Sawm (the fourth pillar) requires Muslims to fast during the holy month of Ramadan. From first light to sundown, Muslims abstain from food, drink and sexual relations.

5. Hajj (the fifth and final pillar) is the pilgrimage to Mecca which all Muslims hope to perform at least once during their lifetime. It is an obligation only for those who are physically and financially able. The Hajj begins in the 12th month of the Islamic year (which is lunar not solar) and closes with the festival Eid al-Adha (which is celebrated with prayers and exchange of gifts). This and the Eid al-Fitr (a feast day commemorating the end of Ramadan) are the main festivals of the Muslim calendar.

Friday is the Muslim holy day and the only day on which men must go to the mosque to pray. Women may attend prayers at the mosque on Fridays or they can pray at home. Both male and female practicing Muslims avoid pork and alcohol.

In the 7th and 8th centuries following Muhammad's death, the Islamic faith spread rapidly through Arabia and neighbouring countries. This was due to Muslim traders and to the expansion by Muslim armies establishing a vast empire from Spain and North Africa to India. Today more than 20% of the world is Muslim and over 1,000,000 Canadians are as well (3.2% of Canadian population).

* The term imam in Islam is not synonymous with priest in the Catholic faith, pastor in the Protestant faith, or rabbi in the Jewish faith. In Canada, someone who leads prayers at a prayer service is temporarily an imam. To become an imam in this sense, one may merely need to be an adult male. The word can also simply mean *leader* and be merely a title of honour. Some Islamic congregations <u>do</u> hire an imam to work in much the same function as a parish priest or rabbi to

help guide the congregation. This person, especially in large centres, is well educated in Arabic and the history of Islam.

13
HINDUISM

Hinduism is one of the world's oldest and most varied religions and enjoys 700 million followers worldwide including 500,000 in Canada (1.5% of the Canadian population).

The true name of the religion of Hindus is 'Sanatan Dharma'. *Sanatan* means ageless (more than 5000 years old) and *Dharma* refers to a specific religious set of rules. Much like the Ten Commandments of the Jewish and Christian faith, the Sanatan Dharma principles were revealed from God. In this case, these rules were revealed to the yogis and ascetics while they were in deep states of meditation as intuitive knowledge from Brahmin (or the Supreme Consciousness).

Hinduism dates back to the time of the great Indus Valley civilization in the Indian subcontinent. Around 2000 BCE, the nomadic Aryan people came over the Caucasus Mountains and invaded what is now India. Their religious ideas mixed with those of the people of the Indus valley to form the basis of Hinduism.

Brahmin (God) pervades all mortal and material objects and incarnates (becomes human) as deities (gods and goddesses). The three principal deities - Brahma, Vishnu and Mahesh - are different projections or manifestations of Brahmin. Only divine beings (deities) can reincarnate as they have the cosmic power to revert back to their original form.

Human beings cannot reincarnate. They, as well as all mortal beings, can only be 'reborn' again and again on their journey to salvation. Hindus believe the soul is recycled into the world in different bodies and who or what you are reborn as depends on your actions in your previous life. This process is known as *karma*. If you lead a good life, you will have a better rebirth and move closer to *moksha*. Hinduism teaches that the soul is perfect, free and unlimited and no matter how many lives are required, eventually each and every soul will reach its divine nature. Once moksha is reached, there is no need to continue to be reborn into further lives. The soul is liberated from suffering and becomes one with the infinite Brahman.

Many Hindus worship in temples. Each temple is dedicated to a particular god or goddess and is believed to be the deity's earthly home. There are no set times or days to go to the temple. As well as worshipping at the temple, some Hindus set aside a small place in their home as a shrine with space for a statue or a picture.

When Hindus visit the temple they usually take off their shoes and women cover their heads as a sign of respect. Hindus visit a temple to pray and to view the statue representing the deity. They may take offerings of the five basic elements (earth, water, fire, air and space) in the forms of food, water, milk or fruit. These gifts are called *puja*. The priest presents the gifts to be blessed, returns them to the devotees and marks their foreheads with a red mark of blessing. This ceremony is known as *prasadam*.

The oldest Hindu sacred texts are the four collections of hymns, prayers and stories called the *Vedas*, which were composed over 3,000 years ago. Other important texts include the *Upanishads* and two long poems called the *Mahabharata* and the *Ramayana*. The *Upanishads* are teachings presented in the form of stories and parables.

There are many Hindu festivals to mark special occasions such as birthdays of the gods and goddesses, harvest time and family events. Many Hindus also make pilgrimages to sacred places such as the city of Varanasi on the banks of the Holy River Ganges. Every twelve years in January or February, millions of pilgrims travel to the banks of the River Ganges at Allahabad to celebrate the *Kumbha Mela*.

Most Hindus celebrate the main festivals of the year - Diwali, Holi and Dessehra. These are lively, colourful occasions where people visit the temple, eat special food and exchange candy and gifts. Diwali is the festival of lights (late October or early November), Holi marks the coming of spring (March or April), and Dussehra (September) marks Rama's triumph over the Ravana.

Hindus may worship one god, many gods or none at all. Most Hindus, in addition to the three main gods, worship other gods and goddesses such as Rama and Krishna – which are incarnations of the God Vishnu. There are no set rules for being a Hindu. One can be a good Hindu and believe in one god, many gods or no gods at all. For Hindus, these contradictory ideas are not seen as a problem. It is only fundamental to believe in *reincarnation* and *karma*.

14
SIKHISM

Often mistaken as a combination of Hinduism and Islam, the Sikh religion is a completely independent faith. Over 20 million Sikhs follow this distinct religion born 500 years ago in the Punjab region of northern India. Between 1469 and 1708, ten Gurus preached a message of truth, devotion to God, and universal equality.

At the time of the birth of Sikhism, the two main religions in India were Hinduism and Islam, but there were deep divisions between the two and many people felt excluded. Guru Nanak, a religious teacher introduced the new religion of Sikhism, which taught tolerance of the faiths.

When Guru Nanak died, his teaching was carried on by nine other teachers, ending with Guru Gobind Singh. It is believed that the ten gurus all had the same soul. Though they had different bodies, Guru Nanak's spirit passed on into his nine successors. While the Sikhs hold their gurus in high reverence, they are not to be worshipped. Sikhs may worship only God.

Sikhs in the World (2011)

(20 million in India)

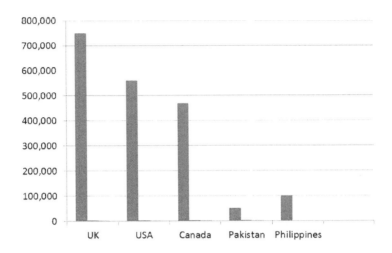

Sikhs believe that there is only one God and they try to remember God in everything they do. This task of remembering is closely linked to the idea of service - doing things for others without thinking of your own reward. By practicing these ideals and following the example set by the gurus, Sikhs hope to grow closer to God.

Guru Nanak preached that in God's eyes, everyone is equal. Followers were encouraged to leave their Hindu caste symbols and take on a common surname: all Sikh men took the surname or middle name Singh meaning lion, and all Sikh women took the surname Kaur meaning princess.

Many Sikhs visit a temple or *gurudwara* to pray. When entering the temple, worshipers must take off their shoes and cover their heads as a mark of respect. They bow in front of the Sikh holy book, the *Guru Granth Sahib*, and sit to listen to hymns read from the scriptures by a male or female reader. When Guru Gobind Singh died in 1708, he told the Sikhs that in the future the sacred scriptures should be their new guru. The scriptures collected together in the *Guru Granth Sahib* were devotional hymns composed by six of the gurus and other holy men.

Devout Sikhs have five symbols of faith known as the Five Ks because they each begin with the letter 'k' in the Punjab language:

1. Kesh (uncut hair) symbolizing obedience to God
2. Kanga (wooden comb) symbolizes cleanliness
3. Kachcha (shorts worn under clothes) symbolizes goodness
4. Kara (stainless steel bracelet worn on right wrist) symbolizes eternity
5. Kirpan (sword) symbolizes strength.

A Sikh must observe and follow a strict code of conduct that includes: worshipping only one God, reciting five prescribed hymns every day, learning the Punjabi language and reading *Guru Granth Sahib*, wearing and observing the significance of five Ks, living a truthful life and treating all humans as equal. Sikhs must not eat kosher meat, smoke, take drugs or intoxicants, or have faith in black magic, superstitions, charms or rituals.

In Sikh scriptures women and men are equal. Women may lead religious congregations, take part in the continuous recitation of the Holy Scriptures, work as a Granthi (ceremonial reader of the holy scriptures, the Sri Guru Granth Sahib, at a Sikh temple) and participate in all religious, cultural, social, and secular activities. Guru Nanak proclaimed the equality of men and women, and both he and the gurus that succeeded him encouraged men and women to take a full part in all the activities of Sikh worship and practice.

15
CHINESE RELIGION

Confucianism is not so much a religion as it is an ethical and philosophical system developed from the thoughts of Confucius. It obtained its stable position under the reign of Emperor Wu of the Han Dynasty (202BC-220AD) and became the ideology of Chinese society in the feudal system.

Confucius (551BC - 479BC) was an educator and idealist. Through his optimism and enterprising spirit, he greatly influenced the character of the Chinese people. He spent his life teaching and helping students solve problems related to noble morals (more than 3,000 students studied under his guidance) and is considered to be the first professional teacher in Chinese history.

His main idea was to administer the country with morals. Regarding personal relationships, he advised others to do not do unto others what you would not want others to do unto you. He advocated the alignment of nature and human beings and suggested that people live harmoniously with nature. He thought that a country should develop its culture and economy at the same time and aimed to establish a world of harmony.

Based on the *Four Books* and *Five Classics*, the traditions and principles in Confucianism play an important role in the formation of Chinese people's thinking patterns. For over two thousand years, Confucianism has guided people's behavior and has been the mainstream of Chinese culture.

Buddhism is an important religion in China. It is generally believed that it was spread to China in 67 AD during the Han Dynasty after being founded 450 years earlier in India. During its development in China, it had a profound influence on traditional Chinese culture and thoughts, and has become one of the most important religions. Typical of the blending of religious thought in China, 30% of the people who do not consider themselves 'Buddhist' have participated in some Buddhist activities. In mainland China, there are about 13,000 temples and 180,000 monks and nuns.

The founder of Buddhism was Siddhartha Gautama, a royal prince born in Nepal about 564 BCE. After many years of prayer and meditation, Siddhartha gained enlightenment, meaning he finally understood the basic truths of life. After his enlightenment, Siddhartha spent the rest of his life travelling around India, teaching and preaching. He soon had a loyal band of followers and was given the title Buddha or 'awakened one'.

Buddha did not want to be worshipped as a God. He taught that people would be happier if they took responsibility for their own thoughts and actions. His teachings were simply a guide for living.
The Buddha's enlightenment had shown him that people suffered because they were never happy with what they had and always wanted more.

They needed to learn new ways of thinking and behaving, so he set out his basic teachings in the "Four Noble Truths":

1. *Human life is full of suffering.* Even death brings no relief because of reincarnation. Salvation or nirvana is to be released from the cycle.
2. *The cause of suffering is greed.* We are too attached to our health, wealth, status and physical comfort. We fall victim to attachment and desire.
3. *There is an end to suffering.* Suffering ends when we cease to crave what we want and cannot have.
4. *The way to end suffering is to follow the middle path.*

The middle path, which lies between extreme luxury and extreme hardship, has eight steps that would lead people to live wiser and more compassionate lives:
1. Right understanding (of the Four Noble Truths))
2. Right attitude (positive thinking)
3. Right speech (not telling lies)
4. Right action (helping others)
5. Right work (doing a useful job)
6. Right effort (doing good things)
7. Right mindfulness (thinking before you speak or act)
8. Right meditation (developing a calm, happy mind).

The Five Precepts (or guidelines) that Buddhists follow in daily life are:
1. do not harm or kill living things
2. do not take things unless they are freely given
3. lead a decent life
4. do not speak unkindly or lie, and
5. do not take drugs or alcohol.

Buddhists believe that sin is the lust that arises in one's life and they seek to rid themselves of lustful desires by self-effort.

Buddha denied that man has a soul and taught that enlightenment was open to anyone including women. He rejected gods as they were unimportant in the quest for enlightenment.

Buddha adopted the Hindu teachings on reincarnation, along with *Karma* and *Dharma*. Buddha taught that one could be reincarnated as a human being, an animal, an angry ghost or a demon. He also incorporated yoga and meditation, which were highly developed skills in Hinduism, directly into his teachings.

Daoism (also recognized or spelled as Taoism) is the last of the three primary movements in the Chinese religion. It is most specifically associated with the *Daode jing* (Tao Te Ching), a philosophical text attributed to Laozi (Lao Tzu) in the 3rd or 4th centuries BCE. The Daode jing defines the Dao as a 'way' or 'path' that identifies the appropriate way to behave. It describes the Dao as eternal (something that pre-existed the creation of the universe). It is the celestial energy from which all forms emerged. Taoism was established as an organized religion by the Way of the Celestial Masters sect, founded in 142 CE. by Zhang Daoling. This group along with later sects of Daoism engaged in complex ritual practices, including devotion to a wide range of celestial divinities and immortals.

In Daoism, a harmonious relationship between nature, humanity, and the divine is emphasized. The key elements are:

- *The One* - the essence of Dao, the essential energy of life, the possession of which enables things and beings to be truly themselves and in accord with the Dao.
- *Wu / Yu* - non-being and being, or not-having and having. Wu also represents the infinite nature of the Dao.
- *Te* - usually translated as virtue or an awareness of the Dao together with the capabilities that enable a person to follow the Tao.
- *Tzu Jan* - that which is naturally so, meaning the condition that something is when permitted to exist and develop naturally without interference.

- *Wu / Wei* – how one follows the Tao, uncontrived action or natural non-action allowing for the unfolding of the natural course.

- *Yin / Yang* - the principle of natural balance between forces, patterns and things that are in relationship and require each other to make sense, opposites that fit together to work in harmony (light and dark, wet and dry, action and non-action, male and female).

- *Ch'i or Qi* - the energy that enables beings to survive and links them to the universe as a whole.

- *Relative Knowledge* – all knowledge is affected by the perspective or the person claiming that knowledge. There is no true knowledge, merely the combination of limitless viewpoints. True knowledge cannot be known - but by practicing the Dao perhaps it can be understood or lived.

Daoism has no centralized authority and different sects have different headquarters. However, the White Cloud Temple in Beijing is a key center for training for priests and for administration. Lacking a central authority along with the underlying belief of relative truth of Daoism has meant the religion has been used politically to support various movements and views.

The practices of Daoism are equally diverse depending on the sect or practitioner. Some of these include: alchemy, recitations of texts, meditation and the spiritual exercise of Tai Chi.

16
DECODING THE RESUME OF A NEW IMMIGRANT

Resumes of culturally different candidates can complicate the goal of matching a position with the best possible candidate. Resumes of recent immigrants may look different than those of native born Canadians so to avoid eliminating a good potential candidate due to an out-of-the-ordinary resume, managers and human resource professionals need to look beyond the resume and decode its unique characteristics to see the value of the candidate.

New immigrants to Canada from Asia come from hierarchical and collective societies and those values are reflected in the resumes they present to Canadian employers. Organizations need to look beyond the face value of these resumes to see what candidates are really saying about their education and experience.

Education – What school and what ranking matters – just not in Canada.

You are considered qualified if you have the minimum specified education requirements. If you have a level of education higher than the required educational level (a master's degree, for example, when a bachelor's degree is asked for) you are even *more qualified* than candidates with just the required educational background.

In Canada, many recruiters would consider a candidate with a master's degree to be *over-qualified* for a position asking for a bachelor's degree, and assume that the candidate would be bored quickly and move on to greener career fields. HR professionals and managers may make the decision to not even interview such a candidate, opting to merely send a letter notifying the candidate that the organization considered him overqualified.

A second issue is that, in many eastern countries, the school you graduate from and your ranking within your graduating class is vital to your employability. Both the schools and your status within the school are rated. For example, out of a graduating class of 250, you may be student number 202. These ratings are taken very seriously in Asian societies because being accepted into a good school and achieving a high rating generally guarantees the graduate several serious job offers upon graduation

Universities in Canada such as Queens University in Kingston, Ontario or McGill University in Montreal, Quebec have some of that cache, but not to the degree that the Indian Institute of Technology (IIT) has in India or the Tokyo University in Japan. Vinod Khosla, ITT alumni and co-founder of Sun Microsystems states, "IIT is probably the hardest school in the world to get into. Put Harvard, MIT, and Princeton together, and you begin to get an idea of the status of IIT in India." IIT only accepts 1% of admissions so many students who wish to attend the esteemed university never do, which also adds to its prestige.

This is why many Asian candidates put their education first on their resume, as opposed to after work experience as many native born Canadian candidates might do. It is also why highly rated graduates from highly rated schools can't understand why they would have to market themselves to an HR recruiter when in their home country they would be the cream of the crop of candidates and be aggressively sought out by organizations.

Experience – What all can you do?

In Canada, we believe that someone is qualified to do a job when they have held similar positions in other organizations. A successful candidate would demonstrate their experience that aligns with the advertised position by detailing their achievements, accomplishments, responsibilities, and results. Canadian managers expect to clearly see this specialization of experience on a candidate's resume. Native born Canadian applicants understand this requirement and tailor their resumes to reflect it.

However, in eastern nations, employees are valued for the ability to see the interconnectedness between business roles and organizational divisions. Transferable skills are highly valued and resumes reflect that spirit. An Asian immigrant's resume will therefore detail all the *different* kinds of experience and skills they may have - leaving the recruiter to interpret that the applicant has breadth but little depth in their field of work. So, unfortunately, even if the applicant does have the depth of experience to master the role, they are perceived as a 'jack of all trades, master of none'.

An Asian candidate may not even have a complete idea as to how to detail accomplishment or achievement in the western business model of job search. Their resumes might list various responsibilities but not necessarily tie accomplishment to those responsibilities, leaving the recruiter to make an educated guess as to the success of the candidate in their home country.

In Asian society, people do not put themselves forward, others do it for them. They find positions through friends, family or through recruiters who solicit them directly from university. In their resumes and interviews, they are expected to highlight group effort over individual achievement. It is characteristics such as these – so valued in the eastern business culture - that can result in an unsuccessful job search in the Canadian marketplace.

To connect with the recruiter 'relationally', candidates from Asia will often include items on their resumes that Canadian HR professionals find inappropriate: marital status, number of dependents, birth date, picture, age, or citizenship. A cover letter might include off-putting salutations or signature lines such as "from your humble servant" or "I pray to God that you will consider my application".

So what can you do to ensure you are attracting the best of the best, in spite of their quirky application ways?

Although the first look at a resume is often brief and cursory, you can alter your process to ensure you identify great candidates by:

- Including on the recruitment *and* selection team staff members that are diverse, particularly from Asian countries
- Looking and asking for evaluations of academic credentials by organizations who compare international education standards
- On your website and social media, explaining your recruiting process, including what you look for on a resume for a position in your organization
- Taking the time to read between the lines where the candidate is attempting to tell you who they are and why they are qualified to be a great new employee for you.

17
THE INTERVIEW: LOOKING BEYOND THE OBVIOUS

All candidates in an interview process are attempting to impress the interviewer with their skills, education and attitude. New immigrants are no different in this desire. However, a new immigrant's way of speaking, gesturing – even sitting – may sabotage their success.

In spite of the candidate's motivation being positive and the interviewer attempting to fairly assess the candidate, cultural misinterpretation may skew the true picture of the candidate's competency. The obvious outcome for the candidate is loss of opportunity or employment, but what is not often considered is the corresponding loss of great talent for the organization.

Let's look at the more powerful misinterpretations:

Handshakes

How do you interpret a soft handshake? Or an extended shake, where the other neglects to release the grip? Or the aggressive squeeze combined with the determined pump?

In everyday business, many people unconsciously determine the confidence and competence of others based on that initial greeting – the handshake.

American business coaches suggest there is a 'normal business handshake' and employees should embrace this standard. However, our workplaces are not composed of a homogenous group of employees who all believe that a low pressure, brief handshake is considered a sign of weakness or a lack of confidence. Neither can we ignore that many Canadians perceive that a longer or stronger handshake is a demonstration of rudeness or aggression. When we receive a handshake even slightly different than or own, impressions are made and misinterpretation may occur.

If a low pressure, very brief, minimum motion handshake is on one end of a continuum, and a longer, stronger pressure, pumping handshake is on the other end, where does your handshake register? If you meet someone and shake their hand and their handshake preference is lower pressure than yours, what do you read into that fact? Alternatively, when you meet someone whose handshake is longer and has more pressure or movement than yours, what does that mean to you?

The handshake is not an international form of greeting, although it has become the universal form of greeting in the North America and northern Europe. Asian immigrants are less likely to have used a handshake as a form of greeting in their home countries. When they do shake hands, immigrants from the four nations of China, India, Pakistan or Philippines are very likely to give a soft pressure, quickly release form of the exchange.

Eye Contact

In many cultures, it is not appropriate to hold eye contact for the same length of time that is considered 'normal' in North American business culture. In East Asian cultures, it is disrespectful to look a more senior person in the eye, but avoiding eye contact in North American culture is often interpreted negatively. Although the person giving the minimum eye contact feels that their behaviour is appropriate, it can be interpreted as suspicious or seen as an effort to dodge truthful disclosure. We even may have said that someone 'wouldn't look me in the eye' to refer to a person who has done something dishonest and is hiding the fact.

Candidates from Asia are more likely to look down, look around the room than look in the eye of the recruiter – whom they see in a senior role or more powerful role than their own.

If a very direct, extensive holding of eye contact is on one end of the continuum, and a very short and quickly diverted holding of eye contact is on the other, where does your preference register? As with handshakes, what do you read into the behaviour that is different than yours?

Space

What do you think about a candidate who sits too close to you? Or distances themselves from you?

When someone 'invades' our space, we feel uncomfortable. We are willing to sit close to someone on an airplane or in an elevator for the necessary length of time to complete our journey. We are willing to take the last stool in the bar, squeezing ourselves between two other imbibers so we can get off our feet. But if there are four open seats next to another person in the airport waiting area, Canadians will respectfully leave at least one seat open between the other person and themselves, sitting in the immediately next space only when necessary.

Alternatively, when someone steps too far out of what we would consider appropriate space, we feel that they are distancing themselves for a reason. We wonder what is the cause of this behaviour we consider negative: Are they trying to distance themselves because they don't wish to be associated with us? Do we have an odor?

We don't often put these space mismatches down to culture, but Asian immigrants and European descent Canadians often do see space in different ways.

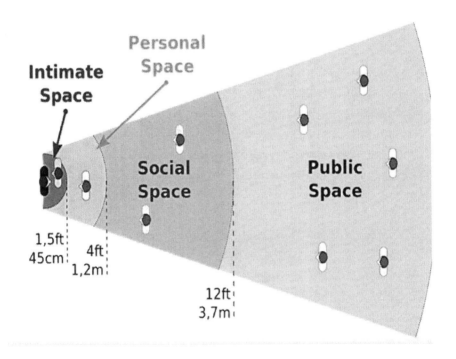

Different cultures have different tolerances for the distance two people sit or stand apart

There is **intimate distance** (used for embracing, touching or whispering) which depending on the culture is less than six inches to a range of 3-18 inches.

Personal distance which is a term we are all familiar with and is used for interactions among good friends or family. In some cultures this is 1.5 feet to 2.5 feet and in other cultures as wide as 4 feet.

Social distance is a term we often mean when we use the term personal space. You may feel comfortable standing across from your spouse or sibling and allowing only two feet between you, but this would seem too close if the other person was just introduced to you. Social distance is used for interactions between acquaintances and in some cultures is 4 to 7 feet and in others as large as 12 feet.

Public distance is used for public speaking and is 12 to 25 feet in close cultures and more in less close cultures.

When a candidate moves closer or sets further distance, before you take offense or make a judgement, think about this unconscious difference. Generally, immigrants from the four immigrant nations of China, Pakistan, India and Philippines have a shorter distance in space definitions above compared to Canadians.

Smiles

Smiling is a confusing behaviour, cross culturally. Canadians often have a smile on their face, regardless if they are amused or not. It is seen as a common welcoming and relationship building strategy. However, in Asia, smiling might also mean embarrassment and a gesture to cover loss of face or humiliation.

Nodding

There is often confusion about what is a nod and what is agreement, particularly from immigrants from India. A head movement back and forth (to the left and right) usually implies disagreement in Canadian culture. But to immigrants from India, this movement could just as easily mean that they agree with what is being said.

You can see how this could lead to miscommunication. To ensure that you are on the same page, verify this body language through spoken language.

Emotion

Many people from East Asia will demonstrate minimum emotion in public. If an interviewer thinks that a candidate should 'show' that the job interests them, they might miss the enthusiasm that is hiding under the surface.

Deference

Immigrants from Asia come from more hierarchical societies, as we will discuss further in later chapters. Due to this perspective, candidates may show more formality than Canadian interviewers and managers may be comfortable with. If they stand until they are told to sit down, insist on letting you go through the door first, or call you Mr. or Ms. – don't see these behaviours as a lack of confidence in themselves. It is their respect for you that is being demonstrated.

Language

In a further chapter on language, we will discuss the impact of accent and silence on communication. Regarding interviews specifically, remember that if English is the candidate's second or third language, they may need to take a few more moments to locate the correct word in English to express themselves clearly. Do not take a pause as a lack of an answer or a lack of ability.

Language is of particular importance in the interview stage and this is also why telephone interviews often make an immigrant seem less competent than they might really be. An interviewer cannot tell over the phone if the candidate is just getting their thoughts in order or if they have no answer. The interviewer only hears the sound of silence, and often downgrades the competency of the candidate.

To ensure when you interview a new immigrant you are getting a true picture of their abilities, consider:

1. Interviewing in person when possible.
2. Recognizing the candidate may make personal comments or ask personal questions in an attempt to build relationship.
3. Moving your chair to re-establish your comfort zone if the candidate sits closer than you would normally find comfortable.
4. Accept any formality with the positive intention that it is extended.
5. In reflection with the previous chapter, push for explanation of what projects the candidate was involved in and their role. (A candidate's natural inclination to discuss everything in the collective must be unbundled if you wish to identify their true individual skills.)

18
COMMUNICATING
HIGH CONTEXT/LOW CONTEXT

"Then you should say what you mean, the March Hare went on.
"I do," Alice hastily replied; "at least I mean what I say – that's the
same thing, you know."
Lewis Carroll, Alice in Wonderland

When a person doesn't mean what they say or say what they mean
or beats around the bush – do you perceive them to be a poor
communicator? Non-transparent? Or worse - untruthful? Your country
of origin may be a fundamental factor in determining whether you are
an explicit (spell it all out) kind of communicator or an implicit (make
me read between the lines) kind of communicator.

Canada, the United States of America and Australia are immigrant
nations. Their national characters are defined as much by the people
who have arrived on their shores in the past 400 years as the

indigenous people who have inhabited the land for thousands of years. Due to this multicultural element and the lack of common understanding that accompanies more homogeneous nations, these three immigrant nations have a 'low-context' for communication. Without a common sense of the world they live in, people from these nations cannot afford to communicate in an implicit or unstated way without a high risk of miscommunication. This lack of context means that for the listener to receive the communicator's message clearly, the speaker must be explicit and precise in their communication.

As we discussed in the chapter on eastern and western thought, Asian societies are more likely to be 'high context' and western societies 'low context'. This dichotomy in style can lead to workplace miscommunication.

Erin Meyer, a researcher and professor at France's INSEAD University, developed a multi-scale model that illustrates areas of cultural difference. In the diagram on the next page based on Meyer's research, you will note that the three most 'low-context' countries are the three immigrant nations – United States, Canada and Australia. The countries on the right are more homogeneous with less immigrant movement interfering in their patterns of thinking and behaving as a culture. You will further notice that the countries to the farthest right on the scale are eastern – China, Japan, Korea and Indonesia. Although Pakistan and Philippines are not on this chart, the Philippines sits slightly to the right of China and Pakistan sits in the same position as India.

Notice that the three most 'low context' countries are the three immigrant nations and the nations Canada is receiving the most immigrants from are on the far end of the continuum - 'high context'. It is easy to see from this chart why there is so much confusion and frustration in a workplace with a highly diverse workforce.

Note on the following pages, charts showing the combination of Canada and China, Canada and India, Canada and Pakistan, and Canada and Philippines regarding this continuum. Look for similar pages in each of the next six chapters.

US	Netherlands	Finland		Spain Italy Singapore	Iran	China Japan
Australia	Germany	Denmark	Poland	Brazil Mexico France	India Kenya	Korea
Canada		UK		Argentina Peru Russia	Saudi Arabia	Indonesia

Low-Context ←→ High-Context

How is low-context and high-context defined in relation to communication in the workplace?

Good communication in a low-context environment is one where the speaker or writer is precise, using simple, specific and clear language – both in words, voice and gesture. Messages are expressed and understood at what is termed 'face value' or 'what I say is what I mean'. Repetition of statements, summaries and clarification questions are seen as key strategies for good communication in this kind of environment.

Good communication, however, in a high-context environment assumes common understanding of what people mean with minimum words or gestures. It is highly nuanced and layered, often with secondary or tertiary meaning beneath the 'face value' message. Messages are implied and the culture of the environment makes explicit communication unnecessary. Communicators look beyond what is being presented on the surface.

Keeping these two definitions in mind, it is easy to understand how irritating it would be if you think in a high context way and someone communicates to you in a low context way. You feel like saying, "I got your point – I don't need to be treated as a child." Alternatively, in a low context society, don't be surprised if someone blurts out, "Quit beating around the bush and get to the point," if you are communicating in a high context way.

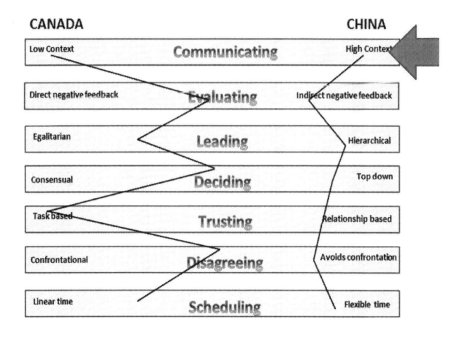

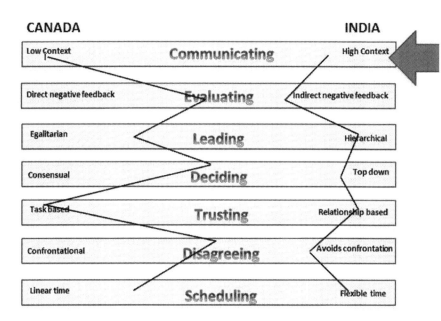

94

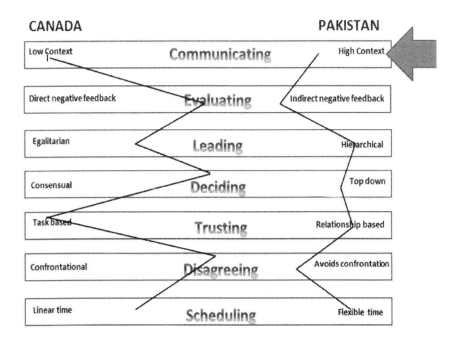

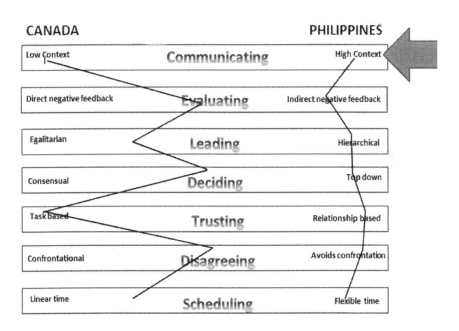

According to Meyer, "… in high-context cultures, the more educated and sophisticated you are, the greater your ability to both speak and listen with an understanding of implicit, layered messages. By contrast, in low context cultures, the most educated and sophisticated business people are those who communicate in a clear, explicit (low context) way. The results are that the chairman of a French or Japanese company is likely to be a lot more high-context than those who work on the shop floor of the same company, while the chairman of an American or Australian organization is likely to be more low-context that those with entry-level jobs in the same organization."

So, well educated immigrants from high context nations may find that managers in Canada seem to 'talk down to them' when they are giving explicit direction. Alternatively, Canadian managers may see new immigrants from high context nations 'don't know what they are doing' because the new Canadians don't 'get to the point'.

Assumption of Motive

In the earlier chapter on how we think, we discussed the equation of B + I + I = T or behavior plus intention plus interpretation equals truth.

For example, Ravi is originally from India, a high context nation. When asked by his Canadian manager, Henry, to complete a project by Friday noon, he replies, "It will be challenging, but I will do my best." This means that Ravi knows it will not get done in time but expects that his manager will read between the lines and understand. When people from India, China or Philippines express an idea or opinion, they expect that the other person in the conversation will take an equal role in the revealing of the message – to co-create meaning. They expect the other to not only hear the words but how it was said and what was not said.

(If Ravi was from a low context nation, he might have replied, for example, "This will not be finished by the deadline. It is just   not possible.") The project is late (according to Henry) when it is not completed by Friday, yet Ravi thinks he communicated clearly that it would be not be finished by the deadline.

Let's break it down:

Behavior: The act of not finishing the job on time

Plus Intention: Henry's possible interpretation of Ravi's intention based on Henry's own motivation if he had the same behaviour (I would only say I would do something if I was going to do it. If I said I would and then didn't complete the work, it would be because I don't respect my manager's request, don't care about the work, or tend to lie to avoid work or cover incompetence.)

Plus Interpretation: according to Henry, being a good employee means doing what you say you will do.

Equals truth: truth according to Henry: Ravi cannot be depended upon to do what he says he will do - which may result in him letting down the team.

When low and high context collides

In Canada (a low context nation), when a manager gives implicit direction, there is a reasonable chance that the receiver of that communication receives a muddled message. That is why we embrace verbal recapping at the end of a meeting, follow up emails to summarize decisions of a conversation, say what we mean and mean what we say. Lack of explicit information or recap of meetings, with specific tasks, time lines and doers assigned, makes low context people unclear and uncertain. This uncertainty can often lead to nervousness about the direction or success of the project or task.

Coaching High Context Employees

As a manager, you need to not only be listening and reacting differently with an immigrant from a high context nation, you need to also move that person to a more balanced communication style with others in your team and organization. Here are four key strategies to share:

- Be specific.
- State your ideas clearly and in a linear format.
- Recap key points.
- Ask for clarification if you are unclear on the message.

High Context to High Context Conflict

If two people are both high context, unless they come from the same culture, there will be guaranteed miscommunication. They are both reading between the lines of the other's communication, but they are reading different lines from different books.

When you have high context employees on your team from different cultures, the best - and only - effective choice is for EVERYONE to focus on the low context behaviours of clear, explicit communication.

Keys to Effectively Listen to a High Context Speaker:

1. Listen to what is between the lines
2. Listen more diligently – both to the words and manner in which they are said
3. Reflect more
4. Paraphrase and ask clarifying questions
5. Be open to the most subtle of body language clues
6. Stop what you are doing and give 100% of your attention to the other person.

19
EVALUATING
DIRECT/INDIRECT NEGATIVE
FEEDBACK

Many managers have been trained to give negative feedback to subordinates using a strategy called the 'feedback sandwich'. In this model, the manager first provides positive feedback, follows it with negative feedback, and finishes up with a dash of good feedback before finishing the conversation.

Several factors have driven the use of this model: a desire to maintain and build the self-esteem of those on our team, a reticence on behalf of the manager to be seen as tough, bullying or unlikeable, and thirdly, particularly in the litigious United States – a reluctance to put oneself or the organization in a position to be sued.

Unfortunately, this feedback strategy often fails. Sometimes it is due to the factor of 'recency' where the employee most strongly remembers the last thing that was said to them – that dash of final positive feedback. Other times, an employee can tell themselves that 'overall' they are doing a good job and are comforted by the positive words that framed the call to action to change their ways. But in the case of an employee who is a new immigrant from a high context nation – the message is simply lost in translation.

Russia		France	Italy	US	UK	Brazil	India	Saudi Arabia	Japan
Israel	Germany	Norway	Australia		Canada	Mexico	China	Korea	Thailand
Netherlands	Denmark	Spain			Argentina		Kenya	Ghana	Indonesia

←——————————————————————————————→

Direct negative feedback   **Indirect negative feedback**

In the previous chapter, we discussed how the communicators in the three immigrant nations of Canada, USA and Australia – all low context nations – have a desire to be explicit and clear when they communicate. It would stand to reason that they would also give positive and negative feedback in a clear and specific way. However, this is simply not so. On the graph above, you will see that Canada has moved considerably to the right of its position on the low context/high context graph - as has the United States and Australia. Canadian managers recognize the need for direct negative feedback - but just don't give it.

The fact that Canadian managers tend to be very specific in communication regarding everything but feedback is puzzling and confusing to new Canadians from eastern nations.

Let us look at how we define direct and indirect negative feedback for the purpose of understanding the following graphs.

Direct Negative Feedback is defined as negative feedback to a colleague or subordinate that is provided frankly, bluntly, and honestly. Negative messages stand alone and are not softened by positive ones. privately, but just as often in front of a group.

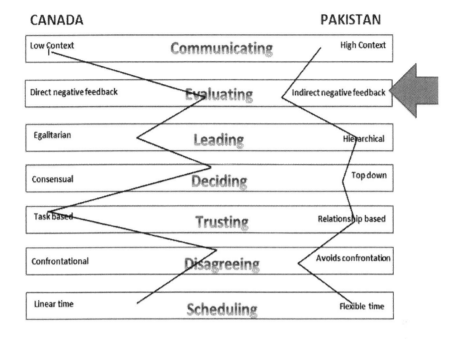

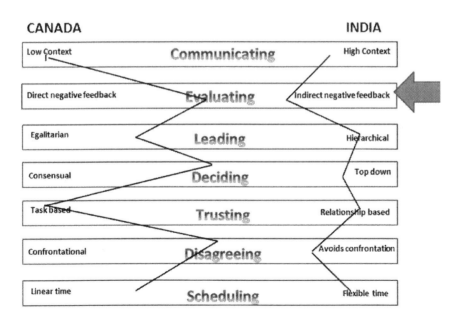

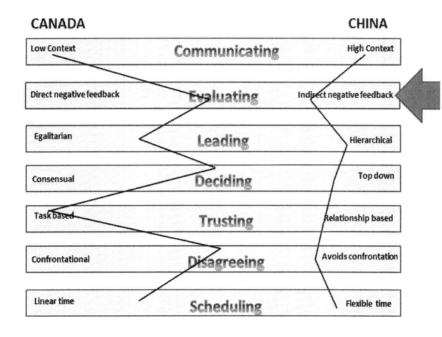

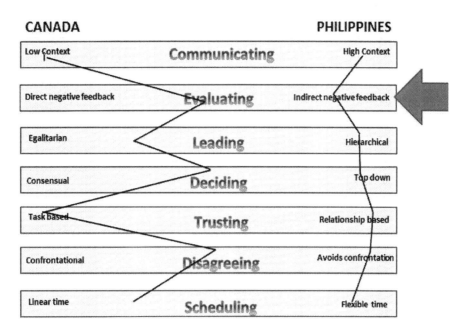

Absolute descriptions are often used when criticizing, such as 'absolutely' or 'totally'. Criticism may be given to an individual

On the right side of the graph, **_Indirect Negative Feedback_** is described as negative feedback to a colleague or subordinate that is provided softly, subtly, and diplomatically. Positive messages are used to envelop negative ones, like bubble wrap. Qualifying descriptors are often used when criticizing, such as 'slightly' or 'marginally'. Criticism is given *only* in private.

Managers generally dislike giving negative feedback. This is only human nature. However by giving implicit, vague, little or no negative feedback, a manager has not given the employee an opportunity to truly learn how they could improve. The manager is also short changing the organization from maximizing the effectiveness of that employee. Even more damaging - this lack of leadership sets up the employee for failure and the organization for possible legal issues.

Positive feedback is given to increase the self-esteem of the employee and to ensure that the employee continues behaviour that the leader has identified as positive. Negative feedback is given to an employee to coach the employee to begin a new behaviour that he or she is not currently exhibiting, or to stop a behaviour that is having negative consequences and impacts.

Positive Feedback Model

Let's discuss a clear positive and negative feedback process that works across all low and high context lines.

Let us begin with the positive feedback process:

1. Describe the behaviour you observed (specifically and when)
2. Describe the immediate consequence of that behaviour.
3. Describe the further impact of the consequence.

For example, *"Yesterday, when you asked everyone for their opinion during the meeting, that led all the members of the group to feel their expertise counted. That positively impacted the team in that they will speak up more often. This helps our organization by increasing the number of new ideas."*

It is describing the ongoing impacts of the behaviour that affects the employee. Often individuals do not realize how their actions impact their team or their organization. You will notice that we first describe the behaviour and then consequences and then impacts. Connecting the behaviour to consequences or impacts for the team is even more impactful for easterners who have a relationship focus over individual focus.

Indirect versus General Feedback

It is vital that you focus on behaviour (what you saw or heard) not vague interpretation, particularly when discussing behaviour you wish to see a person change. "When you interrupted me earlier" is behaviour, "You were rude" is an interpretation of that behaviour. An employee will not connect intellectually with your interpretation of their behaviour, only emotionally. So they feel defensive and badly, but don't understand what they specifically did that they can change.

There is a difference between indirect and general or evaluative feedback.

Here are examples of negative feedback that are indirect/general/evaluative:

INDIRECT: Speaking positively about two projects but not mentioning the troubled third project – this is a 'hint' that work needs to be done or improved on the third project. GENERAL: "You need to get your projects complete."
EVALUATIVE: "You don't have good management of your time."
INDIRECT: Speaking about an environmental or relationship factor to

the actual task – the new website is late. A comment not specific but related may be, "It will be nice to see how well our existing clients can find product information on the new website."

INDIRECT: Customers have complained about the grumpy receptionist and he wants her to smile more at clients when they enter the reception area. An indirect hint may sound like, "We like to have a happy atmosphere here in the front office."
GENERAL/EVALUATIVE: "Try to be more friendly."

Negative Feedback

Positive feedback is given to increase self-esteem in the employee and to ensure that they continue the behaviour that their manager has identified as positive. Negative feedback is given to an employee to ensure that they begin a new behaviour that they are not exhibiting, or stop a behaviour that is having negative consequences and impacts.

To give effective negative feedback, first describe the negative behaviour exhibited by the employee, the behaviour's negative consequences and impacts. The more negative impacts the manager can express, the more the employee will see what they are doing is negatively affecting others.

Next, describe the positive behaviour desired, followed by the positive consequences and impacts to the organization and team of this new behaviour.

Here is an example: "When you automatically discard information from your hard drive, this leads to others not being able to access important data when you are not here. This causes the staff to feel incompetent and our customers to not be well served. Those two outcomes lead to a possible decrease in client retention and job satisfaction. What I would like you to do is leave information accessible to others. This would allow other staff to access information immediately, be more efficient and deliver good service."

Where do you give positive and negative feedback?

A manager may be giving explicit feedback, but may be stumbling on one of the more frequent errors: Where and when to give feedback? In front of a group? In private?

Consider the following guidelines that respect both western and eastern business sensibilities:
1. Always give individual negative feedback privately.
2. Always give group negative feedback to the entire group.
3. Always give group positive feedback to the entire group.
4. Decide whether positive individual feedback is most appropriate in private or publicly.

Many managers have been told of the value of giving praise in front of others. Don't we all love praise publicly? The Oscars? Emmys? Grammys? But if we consider the easterner versus westerner focus on individual achievement versus group achievement, we may find that new immigrants from Asia may prefer a more personal private moment to bask in their manager's gratitude. However, acknowledgement for contribution to the team and the team's success is at best a public spectacle.

20
LEADING
EGALITARIAN OR HIERARCHICAL

In Canada, we consider a good leader someone who gives decision making power to an employee as soon as that employee becomes appropriately competent in their skills and knowledge and confident in their ability to carry out the project or task. Not releasing power to make decisions and take action is often seen as micro-managing – a leadership style which is often derided in the Canadian workplace. Another sign of equality in the workplace is our lack of formality of address. Outside of the political sphere, formality has slowly declined to a casual relationship between superiors and subordinates. Rarely would a manager, except perhaps when involved in a job interview, be addressed as Mr. or Ms.

Canadians often think that all employees want to have as much decision making power as possible and that employees wish to be involved in the decision making process. This egalitarian perspective assumes that, when it comes to leadership and decision making, the ideal distance between a boss and a subordinate is minimal. The best manager is one who acts as a facilitator among equals and the best organizational structures are ones that are flat and where communication is free flowing and not restricted by departmental or hierarchical silos.

Cross cultural researcher, Geerte Hofstde, coined the phrase 'Power Distance' and defined it as "the extent to which the less powerful members of an organization accept and expect that power is distributed unequally'. Countries that have high power distance accept the hierarchical order in which people are in the organization and there is no further justification needed to explain who has power. Therefore inequalities of power and wealth distribution are allowed in the society. On the other hand, countries having low power distance support equality and demand justification for inequalities of power. In these societies, equality and opportunity for everyone is highly reinforced.

Robert J. House of the University of Pennsylvania did a massive research project of 17,300 middle managers in 951 organizations and 62 countries to develop a series of cultural competencies. From his GLOBE study, we can identify the power distance between Canada and our four immigrant nations of China, Philippines, India, and Pakistan.

At a score of 94, the Philippines is definitely a hierarchical society. People accept a hierarchical order in which everyone has a place and everyone accepts their place in that order. Hierarchy in an organization is seen as reflecting inherent inequalities where subordinates expect to be told what to do and the ideal boss is a benevolent autocrat.

At 80 on the power distance scale, China is a society that believes that inequalities amongst people are acceptable. The subordinate-superior relationship tends to be polarized and there is no defense against power abuse by superiors. Individuals are influenced by formal authority and believe people should not have aspirations beyond their rank.

Power Distance

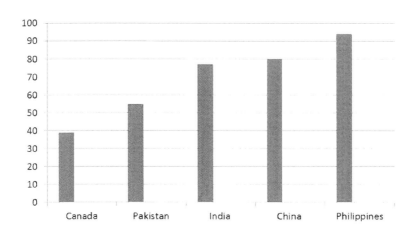

India, at a score of 77, indicates an appreciation for hierarchy and a top down structure in society and organizations. Employees would be dependent on the boss or the power holder for direction and would willingly accept unequal rights between the power-privileged and those who are farther down the organizational chart.

In all three cases above, management directs and rewards in exchange for loyalty and obedience from team members. Communication is top down and directive in its style and often feedback, especially if it is negative, is never offered up the ladder to a superior.

Pakistan has a score of 55 on the power distance index, considerably lower than its neighbor India. This is slightly lower than what has been reported in the research by Meyer on culture mapping. (Note the egalitarian/hierarchy continuum at the end of this chapter and how it varies from the chart above regarding Pakistan.)

With a score of 39, Canadian culture is marked by interdependence among its inhabitants and there is value placed on egalitarianism. This is also reflected by the lack of overt status or class distinctions in society. Typical of other cultures with a low score on this dimension, hierarchy in Canadian organizations is established for convenience with superiors generally accessible and managers relying on individual employees and teams for their expertise. It is customary for managers and staff members to consult one another and to share information freely. With respect to communication, Canadians value a straightforward exchange of information.

So what behaviors does a person from a high hierarchy nation expect?

They expect their boss to separate themselves from their team. So expect to have to explain if you share cubicles with your team members, spend coffee breaks or lunches with your subordinates or act as a coach more than a director. Express that you really do wish to be called by your first name and explain your workplace model for delegating work as competence is demonstrated by the subordinate.

What can you do to move an employee to a more egalitarian perspective?

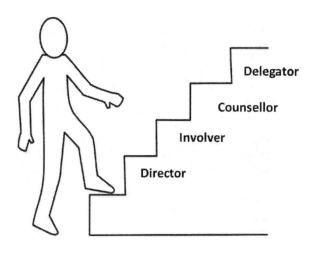

The Staircase Model, as developed in my earlier book, *Escape from Oz - Leadership for the 21st Century,* describes four different leadership strategies of how leaders may communicate with staff members who report to them. It is especially valuable in explaining to a new immigrant how you will move them up a succession of steps to more and more responsibility and that that progression is not only a good thing – but an expected one.

The knowledge and skill set of the employee and the task that is being considered determines which stair of the Staircase Model the leader should be standing on with the employee. Think of the strategies as a flight of stairs with the bottom stair being the narrowest.

The first stair is called **director**, because there is considerable direction that comes from the leader to the employee. If the employee is new to the job at hand or has minimum knowledge, they need to be told what to do, how to do it, when, and why. This may be where many new immigrants are comfortable, but that doesn't mean with some coaching they won't climb the stairs quickly – increasing their effectiveness and productivity.

If a leader moves an employee too quickly up the staircase, it may leave the employee feeling unsupported. It may also make the manager seem like he is abdicating his role.

The second stair involves more responsibility, more decision making and a wider frame of reference. A leader who is communicating from stair two is an **involver**. They involve the employee in making the decision by listening to the subordinate's perspective and ideas and then making the decision.

The third stair is a **counselor** or coach role and is best used once the employee has the skill set and information to make a decision, but still looks to the leader to help clarify decisions before they are made. The leader offers support and asks the employee what he thinks and then coaches him to a decision.

It is at this third stair where the decision making shifts from the leader to the employee - where a leader coaches the employee to a decision, helps the employee to see the missing pieces or plays 'devil's advocate' so the employee can see any cracks in their plan.

The fourth stair is a **delegator** role where the employee has sufficient confidence and competence to carry out the job or task with minimum input or direction.

If a leader leads from the bottom couple of stairs with a highly competent and confident employee, that employee will feel suffocated and micromanaged. If a leader leads from the top couple of stairs with an employee who has little task or organizational understanding, that employee will feel unsupported and see their leader as an abdicator of their role of manager.

Managers have a predominant or preferential way of leading others, a particular stair they wish to stand on. It might be a strategy learned from other managers or leaders who led them in the past. It might have been the first style they latched on when they entered the work world. Regardless of what their current style might be, they need to question whether it is too inflexible.

Leaders often want a simple answer to the leadership question, even though it may not be the most effective. The Staircase Model is based on flexibility and adaptability. Leaders need to be flexible in their strategy and adapt to the needs of the scenario and person they are leading. Focus must not only be on who is being led and their competence and confidence, but on the current situation and the tasks being faced.

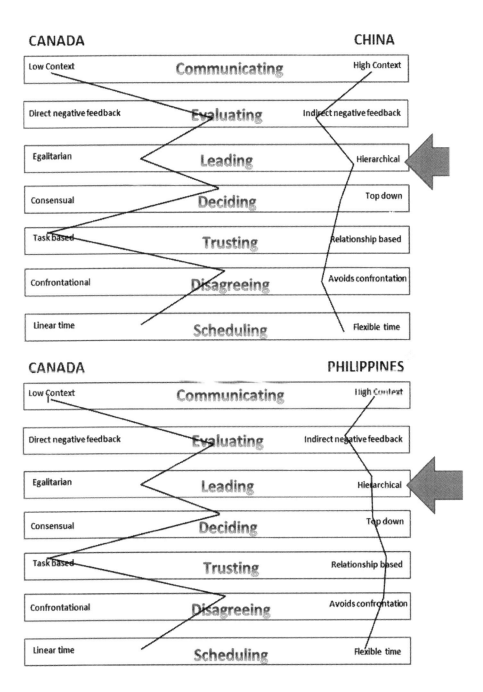

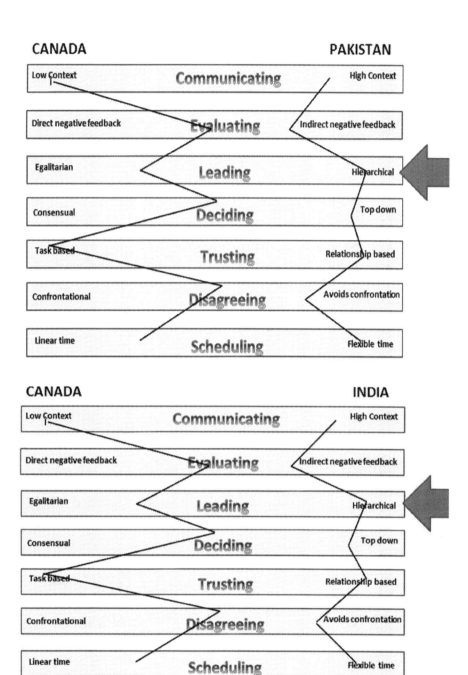

CANADA   PAKISTAN

Low Context	Communicating	High Context
Direct negative feedback	Evaluating	Indirect negative feedback
Egalitarian	Leading	Hierarchical
Consensual	Deciding	Top down
Task based	Trusting	Relationship based
Confrontational	Disagreeing	Avoids confrontation
Linear time	Scheduling	Flexible time

CANADA   INDIA

Low Context	Communicating	High Context
Direct negative feedback	Evaluating	Indirect negative feedback
Egalitarian	Leading	Hierarchical
Consensual	Deciding	Top down
Task based	Trusting	Relationship based
Confrontational	Disagreeing	Avoids confrontation
Linear time	Scheduling	Flexible time

21
DECIDING
CONSENSUAL OR TOP-DOWN

The balance between discussion, debate and decision is one that challenges all teams in Canada. How long do you openly discuss (or brainstorm) before you choose an idea, debate the pros and cons of that idea, make a decision, and then devise a plan to move forward? Does the leader make the decision as a team or does the leader make a unilateral choice and the team members are expected to fall in line with their manager's selection?

Leading a team from an egalitarian viewpoint (where the organizational chart is flat, space is assigned based on use not power, and relationships up and down the ladder are informal) versus a hierarchical point of view (where the manager leads from the front, titles and status rule, and organizational structures are fixed and multi-layered) is not related to how decisions actually get made in the organization or who makes them.

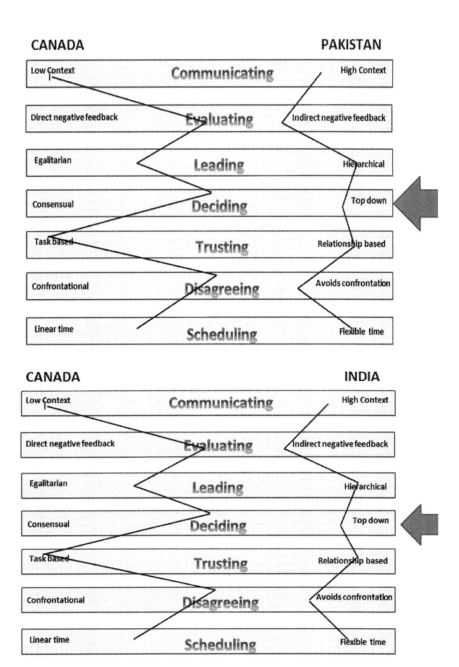

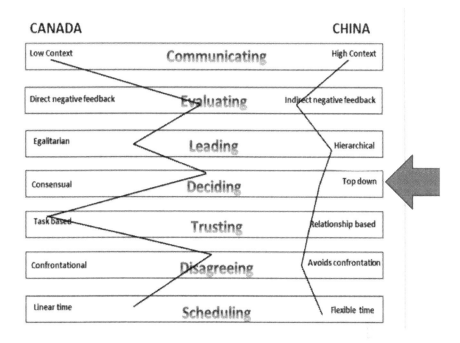

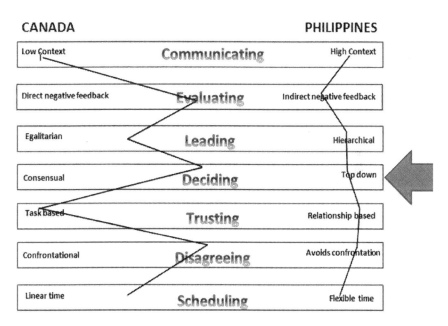

How we make decisions lies somewhere on a continuum from consensual (where decisions are made in groups through unanimous agreement) through to top-down (where decisions are made by an individual - generally the leader of the group).

In most cases, countries that have a hierarchical leadership preference have a top-down decision making style and countries with an egalitarian leadership style have a consensual decision making style. Canada has a more egalitarian leadership preference compared to hierarchical China, Pakistan, India and Philippines. It also has a more consensual decision making style compared to the top-down preference of these four eastern nations.

In a top-down decision making culture, the decision making power is largely held by individuals – the individuals at the top of the team and organization make often unilateral decisions and expect the rest of the team to get on board with that decision.

It is possible that in top-down decision making the leader accesses information and input from many people in their team before making the decision. But in top-down decision making – at the end of the process - it is the decision of the leader that is followed.

It is possible, as well, that consensual decision making does not work as well as one might think. Especially in face to face or telephone exchanges, the process can be high-jacked by extroverted members of the team who get their ideas out first compared to introverts who want time to think about the idea before speaking up or immigrants who may be struggling to choose the best word or turn of phrase.

If you have leaders on your team from the four eastern nations who have subordinates that are Canadian born (especially from a western European background), they will need to be coached as to the best way to bridge to a more consensual leadership style - or they may be perceived as tyrants who don't listen to their team. Coach them to:

- Expect the decision making process to take longer than you might be used to and that there will be additional meetings to get to the final decision. This extended process may try your patience but don't be discouraged – eventually a decision will be made.
- Connect with your colleagues on the same project frequently to demonstrate commitment to the process and to remain in the loop of information.
- Once a decision is finally made, it will be difficult to change so ensure that you input fully with your ideas and information at the beginning and throughout the process.

Keys for a team leader with members from both consensus and top-down decision making nations:

Discuss and agree upon a decision making method at the beginning of your collaboration as a project team. Consider:

- Should the decisions be made by a vote? The team manager unilaterally? Or the team manager after input and discussion by the group?
- Is 100% agreement required?
- Will deadlines for decision be imposed?
- Can decisions be revisited and if so, what is the process?

22
TRUSTING
TASK OR RELATIONSHIP BASED

Do you …

A) develop trust between yourself and another person based on business related activities? Do your work relationships begin easily and then dropped just as easily once the other person is out of your work unit or organization? Do you trust another based on the good work they do consistently? Do you trust someone if they are reliable in their work habits? Do you try never to mix business with pleasure? Do you feel uncomfortable referring a competent person because he or she is a friend?

or do you …

B) trust someone you work with based on how you spend time together that is not just focused on business tasks and priorities? Do you trust others because of the relationships you have developed with conversations around the water cooler, during your coffee breaks, or even while sharing a beverage at the end of the day? Did your trust with each other develop over time? Do you believe that if one of you left the organization to go elsewhere, your relationship would continue beyond that separation?

If you answered yes to more questions in the first paragraph than to the second, you may have an evidence or task-based way of building trust with others. If you answered yes to more of the questions in the second group of questions, you may be from a relationship-based society when it comes to building trust.

Cognitive trust is based on the confidence you feel in another person's achievements, skills and reliability. This is trust that is based on what we 'think', 'experience' or 'observe' and is built on our communication through business interactions. When we each do our work well - we show through our tasks that we are courteous, reliable, consistent, intelligent and transparent. I trust you and you trust me.

Affective trust arises from feelings of emotional closeness, empathy and sympathy for each other, even friendship. This type of 'feeling' trust comes from shared laughs and personal time spent together where experiences are shared and personal information disclosed.

Canadians trust non-business friends and family primarily through affective trust, while they generally gain trust in work colleagues through cognitive trust.

As you can see in the cultural graphs, Canada as a society is much more task-based than are the countries of India, China, Pakistan and Philippines. These four latter nations have a strong relationship-based way of developing trust and that does not bode well for Canadian managers unless our leaders can understand the differences in these two continuums and mitigate the effects.

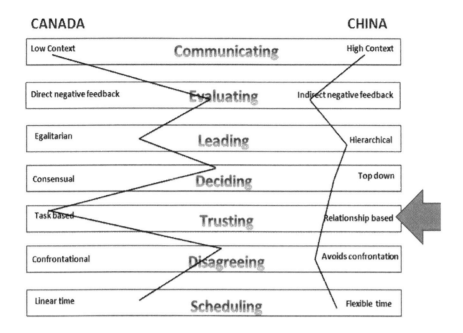

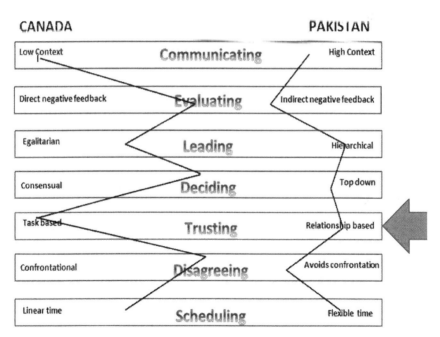

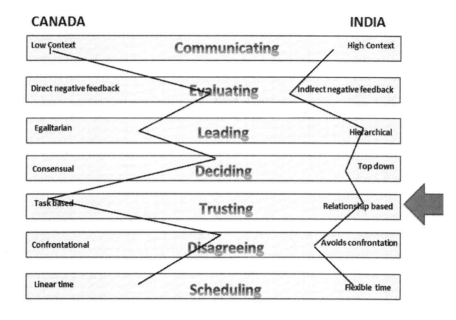

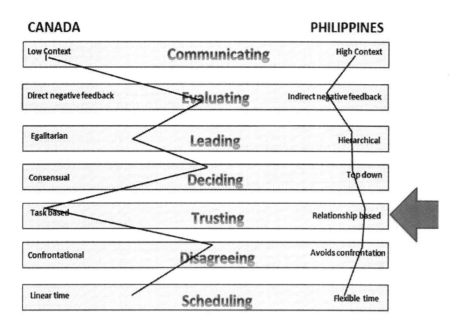

Effect #1 – Canadians appear superficial.

On airplanes, in doctor's offices, sitting at the bar in a hotel lounge on a business trip – all of these situations can lead to the quick and friendly, yet highly personal, conversation that North Americans are known for. We smile at each other on the street and spend polite chatter with each other while waiting for some other part of our life to continue. These short, sometimes intense, but often meaningless conversations often lead nowhere and our lack of follow through from these initial contacts is what simply baffles a person from a relationship-based society.

In a relationship-based society, relationships are built slowly over time and once the relationship is solid, the participants have great loyalty. A leader who manages to develop this kind of trust with his team members can count on their loyalty and support long term – even to the extent of moving to another organization if he does and asks them to do so as well.

Effect #2 – Just the facts

People from relationship-based societies find it difficult to trust others with whom they have no relationship. Relationships are built a little at a time, before meetings, in emails and over the phone. When we connect with someone, we initially spend a period of time in social talk. What is different between relationship-based trust and task-based trust is the time that elapses in that activity.

Here is an example of the little difference you might see in a relationship versus task based exchange.

Consider this telephone call:

"Hello Martin, Jack here. I have a report I need to have disseminated down to your team."

versus

"Hello Martin. Jack here. How did that game go with your son last night? I think you mentioned he was pitching for the first time?" After listening to Martin's answer, "Why I am calling is about a report I need to have disseminated down to your team."

Consider this email:

Martin,
There has been an extension for our report granted for two further weeks.
FYI
Jack

versus

Good morning Martin,
I hope that you had a nice time with your wife yesterday at the BBQ. There were many people there so I was surprised that we bumped into each other!
I have had good news from the director – there has been an extension granted for our report. It is now due in four weeks instead of the two we were anticipating.
Jack

Not only do people from relationship-based societies expect others to develop relationships with them, they expect that the power of relationships will shape their business and career. For example, if two people have a relationship, they will emails from each other immediately. Alternatively, if I don't have a relationship with you, your email might languish in the unopened.

If we work together and one of us gets fired, the relationship is more important than the workplace and loyalties lie within the relationship more so than loyalty to the organization. If we are both from a relationship-based society and have a considerable level of trust between us, not only an I concerned about you losing your job, I would feel an obligation to contact people I know to ensure that your unemployment window is short lived.

23
DISAGREEING
CONFRONTATIONAL OR AVOID
CONFRONTATION

Do you feel hurt or get insulted when someone questions your idea or perspective, especially in public? Or can you get into a lively exchange over any number of topics with others who hold drastically different perspectives? After the dust clears, do you have any bruised feelings - or is the exchange seen as a valuable intellectual exercise from which truth emerges? Whether you embrace or avoid confrontation makes a difference in how you relate to others in your workplace - and your preference may very well be culturally derived.

One of the continuums on Meyer's scale of different cultural paradigms is 'Disagreement'. Canada sits on the fence in this area while the societies of China, India, Pakistan lean towards avoiding confrontation. Philippines as a nation firmly holds on with a tight

CANADA   PAKISTAN

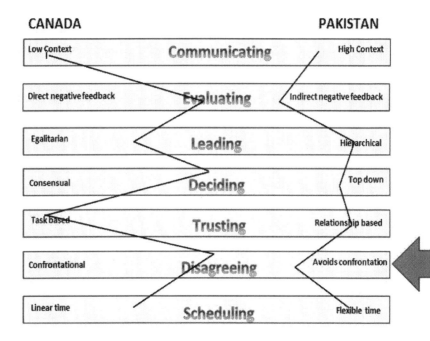

Low Context	Communicating	High Context
Direct negative feedback	Evaluating	Indirect negative feedback
Egalitarian	Leading	Hierarchical
Consensual	Deciding	Top down
Task based	Trusting	Relationship based
Confrontational	Disagreeing	Avoids confrontation
Linear time	Scheduling	Flexible time

CANADA   INDIA

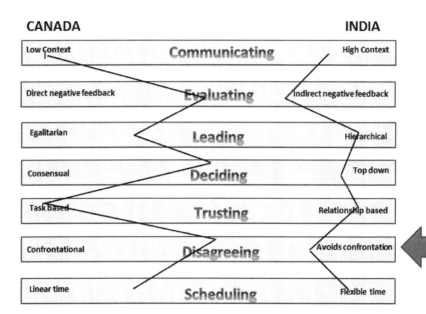

Low Context	Communicating	High Context
Direct negative feedback	Evaluating	Indirect negative feedback
Egalitarian	Leading	Hierarchical
Consensual	Deciding	Top down
Task based	Trusting	Relationship based
Confrontational	Disagreeing	Avoids confrontation
Linear time	Scheduling	Flexible time

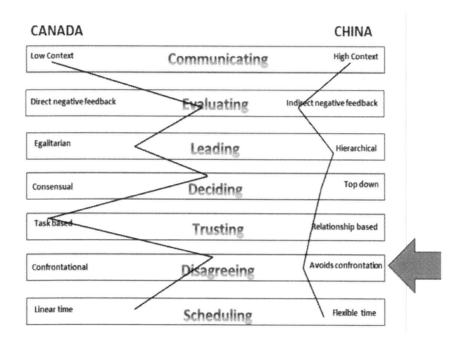

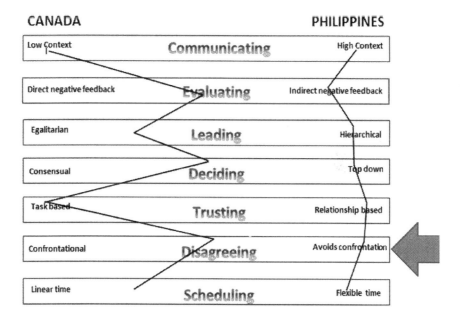

grip to the right edge of the chart with a very strong preference for avoidance.

Communicators who avoid confrontation and communicators who embrace confrontation can relate differently in the workplace and leaders who understand which style the employee prefers can avoid misunderstandings - whether it is between themselves and their subordinates or defusing issues between their multicultural staff members.

In the far left position is *Confrontational* – a strategy defined as when debate is seen as positive for the team and organization. Open confrontation is perceived as appropriate and having no negative impact on relationships.

On the other end of the continuum lies the strategy *Avoids Confrontation*. This position sees disagreement and debate as negative for the team and organization. Open confrontation is seen as inappropriate, a risk to group harmony, and having a negative impact on relationships.

From the diagrams in this chapter, it is clear that Canada is mid-center on this continuum. Pakistan and India are more likely to avoid confrontation, followed by a higher preference for China and then at the extreme right - Philippines. It is not that Filipino society avoids confrontation - they just have an extreme position as to its value. It is important for managers to be aware that if you have Filipino staff they are unlikely to disagree with you or a teammate in public. This could lead to lost opportunities or errors not being identified. You may even find yourself throwing up your hands once the damage has been done and crying, "Why didn't you just speak up?"

Canadians, particularly Anglo-Canadians, are not as far left on this continuum as some nations are - but they are considerably more confrontational that the four countries we are focusing on in this book. For example, it is not uncommon for Canadians to avoid the topics of religion and politics - as they perceive these areas to be ripe for confrontation and high emotions.

In societies that avoid confrontation, it can be considered impolite to challenge people because it is seen as discrediting another person's idea or point of view publicly. Even the slightest difference of perspective should be made as a hint rather than explicitly – and definitely not in an argumentative or aggressive posture. This will lead to a loss of harmony - which is valued higher than progress or efficiency.

In extremely confrontational cultures, where it is natural to attack the opinion or idea of another, there is little concern that the person himself is being attacked. But in an extreme confrontation avoidance culture, the ability to separate attack of an idea and attack of a person is less clear. When my idea is attacked, I am attacked.

In societies that embrace confrontation, especially in the western countries with our individualistic way of seeing the world, it is expected that people will have ideas different than teammates. An ability to discuss, debate and decide in an efficient and productive manner is an expected skill as a good communicator. Ideas need to be dissected and explored and 'group think' avoided at all costs.

We have even created processes to ensure that we explore ideas fully, such as de Bono's Six Hats process and embracing the role of the Devil's Advocate.

The Devil's Advocate

The Devil's Advocate was at one time an official position within the Catholic Church. This person argued against the sainthood or canonization of a candidate. Their role was to uncover any flaws in character or misrepresentation by those advocating for canonization. Today, the term describes someone who takes a position different from the accepted norm or different than the position currently being advocated. This is done for the sake of debate, to explore the idea further, or to unveil potential flaws in an idea.

This role is seen clearly in the position of the black hat in de Bono's Six Hats thinking model.

Six Thinking Hats

Six Thinking Hats is a tool designed by Edward de Bono for group discussion involving six colored hats. Each hat is associated with a way to think about the idea.

Blue – What is the subject? What is the goal? How does this tie to the big picture or our mission?
White – What information is available? What are the facts? What don't we know?
Red – What are our gut reactions to this idea? How do I feel? How do others feel?
Yellow – What are the benefits of this idea? What is great about it?
Green – Where will this idea lead? How does it harmonize with current ideas?

And lastly, the cautious Black Hat. How is this even practical? What could go wrong? What are the potholes in the path of this idea? Is it even realistic?

When Canadians say, "Well let me be the Devil's Advocate for a moment." Or, "if I put my thinking hats on, my black hat makes me ask ...", it means that although they know they must discuss and debate, they are very cautious about bringing up the topic at all if it concerns confrontation. Hence Canada's location on the continuum.

Caveats

There are two caveats to the information above, one related to emotion and one related to trust.

First, emotion itself is not a sign of embracing or avoiding confrontation. For example, immigrants from China tend to be less emotionally expressive than immigrants from Philippines. Yet immigrants from the Philippines are likely to avoid confrontation more than immigrants from China.

Secondly, a person who comes from a high avoidance culture might actually behave against type as described in this chapter in certain situations. This depends on their society's positon on the trust continuum of task versus relationship.

For example in the Chinese culture, a person may avoid confrontation with those he or she is in relationship with, but the more unfamiliar the stranger, the higher the willingness to be confrontational. This is because there is no relationship risk.

Why do you hold a meeting?

Is it to make a decision? Is it to discuss and debate various ideas? Is it to formally approve the decision that has already been decided in informal meetings or discussions?

You may be surprised that most Asians choose the third as the reason for a meeting. They have an expectation that all the discussion and debate will happen in an environment or through a process where there is no risk of having to challenge a person to their face. As there is a close connection between respect for person and respect for that person's idea, denigrating or challenging one means denigrating or challenging the other.

So how can a leader increase healthy disagreement with a team of members with confrontational avoidance societies?

1. If you are the boss, let your team meet without you. They might be more willing to be confrontational and express their disagreement without you present.
2. Give advance notice of the meeting and the type of ideas or inputs you may want from the team members.

3. Depersonalize the ideas from the author of the ideas. Gather ideas or feedback anonymously so team members can disagree with each other without losing face.
4. Avoid giving your idea first - unless of course you just want everyone to agree with you.

24
SCHEDULING
LINEAR OR FLEXIBLE TIME

A colourful, well-worn public bus rumbles down a dusty, nearly deserted road on a Caribbean isle. The vehicle stops to take on the lone woman standing there impatiently.

"You are late!" says the woman.

"I am not late!" says the bus driver.

"You are 43 seconds late!" replies the passenger, pointing at her watch.

A head pops down from a man riding atop of the bus, *"You are now a whole minute late! I will be late for my appointment!"*

Behind the bus, a traveler on a bicycle is brought up short by the stopped bus, *"Oh no, mon,"* he cries, *"Total grid lock!"*

This television commercial for Malibu Rum no doubt makes you chuckle. Many Canadians probably chuckled at it as well. But why

137

chuckle? What is amusing? If the scenario were in Toronto or Vancouver, the conversation would not have been amusing; it would have been real life: people in a hurry, people running late, people not respecting each other's time. Why do we accept and expect adherence to time to be flexible in the Caribbean or Mexico, but not in our own Canadian organizations?

"The real answer was given only in this century by Einstein, who said, in effect, that time is simply what a clock reads. The clock can be the rotation of the earth, an hourglass, a pulse count, the thickness of geological deposits, or the measured vibration of a cesium atom." I.I. Rabi, the Columbia University Nobel Laureate

Up until 200 years ago, most non-Aboriginal Canadians were living much as their ancestors had lived when they first came to North America. They fished and farmed. The people were closely bound to the dynamics of agricultural rhythms, tides, weather and seasons. In Canada, not many people had clocks but everyone was acutely aware of time's passage, especially in nature. In that intensely agricultural society, rural life was unending hard work and operated under deadlines imposed by growing seasons, approaching darkness, and unfavourable weather. "Making hay while the sun shines" was taken literally.[1]

In Europe, massive urbanization had begun and many Europeans moved from rural locations to cities to work in industry. Economic pressures of industrialization required them to become aware of time as a value.

As Canadians began to urbanize, the pressure of the clock came to visit them as well. Agricultural environmental pressure eventually gave way to smaller increments of clock time as the clock became the tool of industrial taskmasters.

In northern Europe and North America, industry brought a fondness for time that was not embraced by the other countries of the world and timeliness was adopted as a virtue. The protestant work ethic dominant in the New World lived parallel with the clock-watching paradigm. Being 'on time', not 'wasting time', using every minute available for productivity became virtuous, as the following quotes illustrate.

"Remember that time is money."
Benjamin Franklin[2]

"A woman is under obligation to so arrange the hours and pursuits of her family as to promote systematic and habitual industry; and if, by late breakfasts, irregular hours of meals, and other hindrances of this kind, she interferes with or refrains from promoting regular industry in others, she is accountable to God for all the waste of time consequent in her negligence."
Catherine Beecher, A Treatise On Domestic Economy, 1841[3]

All time is not the same

Every culture has different ways of organizing time. Some cultures are rigidly bound by their schedules and while other cultures have a relaxed attitude about plans and promptness.

Flexible (polychronic) time stresses involvement with people and completion of transactions rather than an adherence to a preset schedule. Project steps are approached in a fluid manner, changing tasks as opportunities arise. Many things are dealt with at once and interruptions accepted. The focus is on adaptability - and flexibility is valued over organization. Appointment start times are a general or approximate meeting time.

With **linear (monochromic)** time, project steps are approached in a sequential fashion, where one task is completed before beginning the next. One thing at a time. No interruptions. The focus is on the deadline and sticking to the schedule. Emphasis is on promptness and good organization over flexibility. Time is tangible and concrete.

North Americans generally have a monochronic time orientation and for most, time is money - to be used, saved and spent. North

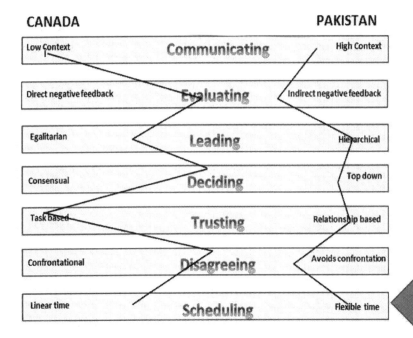

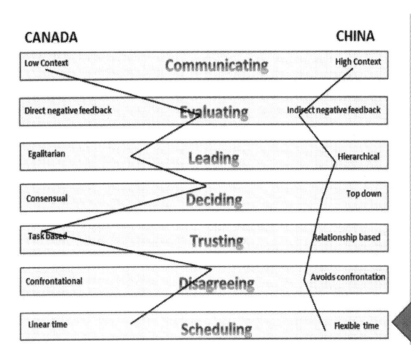

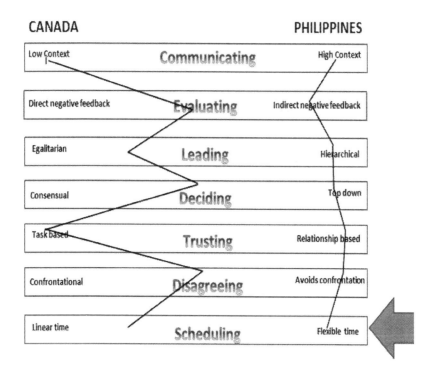

CANADA   PHILIPPINES

Low Context	Communicating	High Context
Direct negative feedback	Evaluating	Indirect negative feedback
Egalitarian	Leading	Hierarchical
Consensual	Deciding	Top down
Task based	Trusting	Relationship based
Confrontational	Disagreeing	Avoids confrontation
Linear time	Scheduling	Flexible time

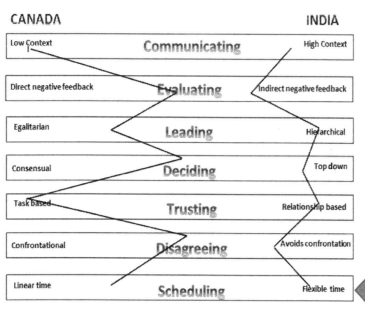

CANADA   INDIA

Low Context	Communicating	High Context
Direct negative feedback	Evaluating	Indirect negative feedback
Egalitarian	Leading	Hierarchical
Consensual	Deciding	Top down
Task based	Trusting	Relationship based
Confrontational	Disagreeing	Avoids confrontation
Linear time	Scheduling	Flexible time

Americans set schedules and appointments and tend to prioritize events and move through the process 'controlling' the time allotted for each part of the process.(4)

In flexible/polychronic countries - which China, Philippines, India and Pakistan are - there is a flexible attitude towards time. Although it is important to be on time for very important appointments, one should always expect to wait, as a meeting may not end simply because the next scheduled appointment has arrived.

In Canada, we may recognize the difference in how time is perceived, yet we usually see monochronic time as good or best and polychronic time as bad. We use words such as 'siesta' time, 'Indian' time, 'East Indian' time, 'island' time, and 'Caribbean' time (often in derogatory ways) to describe those on polychronic/flexible time. This is why we find ourselves amused by the Malibu Rum commercial. The humorous attempt to overlay 'island' time with linear time is what makes us chuckle. Most Canadian workplaces function in the monochronic time mindset and Canadians generally have little patience with those with a polychromic timeset.

Time is A Different Language

If the Asian countries of India, Pakistan, Philippines and China are flexible time societies, then Canada is definitely a linear time society. When our team is comprised of Canadian born members of European descent and immigrants from Asian countries, this scheduling continuum is important to understand. You literally may be speaking different languages.

Anthropologist Edward Hall describes time as a language. It is not enough to say to someone from a polychromic time perspective to be on time. What does being on time even mean? Time is like a language and until someone has mastered the new vocabulary and new grammar of time and can see that there really are two different systems, no amount of persuasion is going to change our 'time' behaviour.(5)

Basic systems such as monochronic and polychronic time patterns are like oil and water and do not mix under ordinary circumstances. In a scheduled dominated monochronic culture as Canada, ethnic groups which focus their energies on relationships find it difficult to adjust to the rigid schedules and tight time processes.

So does your group flex to the flexible preference of Asian team members, or do you drag the Asian team members over to a more rigid process? Neither is the whole answer.

1. Clarify with your team what time means regarding starting and ending tasks and meetings.
2. Be flexible when there are interruptions, from within the meeting or from an outside person. Is the interruption worth adjusting the agenda?
3. Be flexible in your ability to extend time to adjust for the completion of a task, not just the completion of the time allotted to the task at that moment.

25
LANGUAGE

"Why can't he just learn English?"
"Her accent is so difficult to understand."
"He uses the wrong words for things."
"It is so frustrating trying to communicate with a new Canadian!"
"Sure he is brilliant, but I have to repeat what I say over and over again."
"She switches back to her other language as soon as we go on break. Isn't that rude."
"She never says anything."

If you have heard any of the above comments, or said them yourself, you are fully aware that language and accent play a big part in the integration of new immigrants into the workplace and in Canadians acceptance of a diverse workforce.

How do you identify what is beneath comments like these and how can a manager mitigate language driven issues on his team?

145

"Why can't he just learn English?"

A century ago, Asian immigrants came to Canada to work as labourers. They were less likely to have professional education or English language skills. Today, it is a much different picture. Immigrants as a group have more education than Canadians as a group and 93.5% of immigrants speak English or French.

Consider:
- English has slowly become one of the business languages of the Indian subcontinent (India, Pakistan, Bangladesh, Nepal and Sri Lanka) and is the language of the cultural and political elite. 49% of Pakistanis speak English and the official and educational language of Pakistan is English. 130 million Indians speak English. Although this is a small number compared to overall population of India, it is usually the English speaking, educated citizens who leave to find a better life in Canada.
- Of 1200 million people in China, 100 million are English users (a further 300 million are considered learners of English but as of yet could not work in the language).
- 92% of Filipinos speak English.

It is untrue that immigrants are not focused on learning English. Not only do 93.5% of immigrants have working or business level use of the English language, many continue to study towards developing their skills in English and minimizing their accent from their home country.

"Her accent is so difficult to understand."

We don't realize that we all have accents when we speak English.

Twenty years ago, I was travelling with a colleague in Glasgow, Scotland. Although her parents were Canadian born, my friend's father's family still lived in Scotland. On a free day in our schedule, we took the train to visit her family and stayed for afternoon tea. Afternoon tea in Scotland usually means tea and scones with cream and jam - and we weren't disappointed.

After a few cups of tea, I excused myself to use the washroom and when I returned to the sitting room, there was a brief moment of silence. The kind of silence that follows a conversation about the person who is absent. On the way back on the train, I asked my colleague what the conversation had been about just before I returned to the group.
She laughed and said, "My aunt said, "Vicky dear, we can understand you clearly. But your friend, Jeanne has such a thick Canadian accent I could hardly understand a word she said."
Although in Canada, I am used to people understanding my prairie English accent, I never realized that it was indecipherable elsewhere."

(Jeanne Martinson – author)

In western Canada, we acknowledge that citizens from Newfoundland and Labrador speak differently than we do in the western provinces There are even a few words that are spoken differently in the Ottawa Valley compared to the Alberta Rockies. We shouldn't be surprised that as distance increases, different accents do as well.

"He uses the wrong words for things."

Even if our accent is not an obstacle, the words themselves and how we use them can create misunderstandings. We can become aware of our language differences even in a country where English is the first language.

Consider this English speaking Canadian and English speaking Brit:

The Brit might say, *"Let's meet at my office tomorrow at 10 a.m. Conference Room A on the first floor is available."* He then gives the Canadian the building address.

The Canadian arrives at the address the next morning at 10 a.m. and looks around the main floor for Conference Room A. He is unsuccessful and after 15 minutes gives up and goes back to his office. The Brit calls him at noon, inquiring as to why the Canadian missed the meeting.

"I was there," the Canadian huffs. *"I looked around the main floor for 15 minutes but there was no Conference Room A."*

"No, I said the first floor, not the main floor."

"The main floor is the first floor."

"Not in this country!"

English has more words than any language in the world. Those words often have more than one meaning as you see above, depending on context. They often have more than one way to pronounce the same letters. It is a complicated system that defies grammar and logic. If it was logical, words like cough, bough, though, and through would all rhyme.

"It is so frustrating trying to communicate with a new Canadian!"

Language barriers frustrate both communicators. In the television show 'Amazing Race', American teams of two race around the world, following clues and completing tasks that explore the local culture and customs. Watching the competitors race from Rio to Oslo is a great armchair adventure for viewers. What is also interesting are the reactions of the adventurers as they come face to face with culture shock and language issues along the way to the prize. Often the wrong information is communicated with disastrous results for the productivity of the team.

As the players try to communicate through different languages, accents and language patterns, their frustration is apparent. But the locals are frustrated as well as they try their best to help the players

148

complete their tasks. The communication barrier is plainly a struggle for both sides.

"Sure he is brilliant, but I have to repeat what I say over and over again."

Many Filipinos in health care were taught using English language textbooks and were lectured by English speaking professors, but still find some Canadian words incomprehensible.

Sometimes it is the accent of the speaker. Sometimes it is a new word or a word used in an unfamiliar way. Instead of speaking louder (which seems to be the usual response to a request for repetition), if the speaker re-words the point, the listener may catch the meaning in another way.

"She switches back to her other language as soon as we go on break. Isn't that rude."

Speaking a second language is exhausting for most people. Until you know a new language so well that you think in it, you go back in and forth in your head translating. This requires effort and takes time. This is partly why many people speaking English as a second language take longer to respond – they have to think through the question twice.

When a person who speaks English as a second language is speaking to someone who shares their first language, it is natural and relaxing to flip back to that core language. This might be seen as excluding others who might be in the area, but they should not assume the behaviour is motivated by negative or exclusion driven reasons. Sometimes it isn't about you.

Another reason why two people might speak their core language around others who don't understand it is for clarity. If two people both speak English as their second language and Mandarin Chinese as their first, it is only logical - and perhaps even more efficient - to speak in their core language when working together.

"She never says anything."

Sometimes cultural miscommunication occurs not in the talking but in the silence. When new immigrants seemingly disconnect from the conversation or contribute only marginally, this may be misinterpreted as a lack of contribution, commitment, even interest.

This behavior may have other roots than language. Perhaps this person is an introvert and simply isn't inclined to jump in like an extrovert might, or perhaps this is a western-eastern difference.

According to Confucian sage Lao Tzu's, "He who knows does not speak. He who speaks does not know." Many westerners find that talking clarifies what they are thinking - it is hard to know what you think unless you discuss it with like-minded colleagues. Many easterners believe that talking is not thinking and actually works against problem solving.

Researcher Heejung Kim decided to explore whether there was an eastern-western difference in how people use silence and verbal contribution in problem solving. In preliminary research, she found East Asians believed that talking interferes with thinking, while Americans of many ages and professions thought that talking was good for thinking. Kim set up a research project to discover the answer.[1]

She asked life-long English speaking American students to take a non-verbal intelligence test called the Raven Progressive Matrices. Half the students had a European ancestry and half of the students had Asian ancestry (Korean, Chinese, Vietnamese, Japanese). All of the students completed the first half the the intelligence test in silence and the second half while thinking out loud and verbalizing their problem solving process.

The Americans with European ancestry performed better when they were solving the problems while speaking. In contrast, the Americans with Asian ancestry performed much worse when they solved the problems while thinking out loud.

But when the Americans with Asian ancestry were allowed to solve the problems in silence, they performed better than the

Americans of European ancestry. So for Asians, silence is not a sign of checking out, it actually produces their best thinking.

What can you do as a manager to increase language fluency on your team?

Recognize that:

- Everyone has an accent.
- Language barriers are tough on participants on both sides of the conversation.
- It takes extra time and energy to speak in a second language.
- Pausing or silence does not mean the person doesn't know or care.

Speak with clarity, which means:

- Eliminate your metaphors – no 'running something up the flagpole', 'seeing what the cat dragged in' or 'once in a blue moon'.
- Watching your linking of words verbally – a common speaking habit of lazy English speakers - "I am" shouldn't sound like "I yam".
- Pronounce your words clearly and speak slower than you may usually do. By separating the words more distinctly, you assist in everyone's comprehension.
- Encourage others on your team to follow these suggestions for clarity. You will be surprised how the general language clarity of your team increases.

26
WHAT ABOUT AFRICA?

When considering continuums of cultural difference, how does the business culture differ amongst the eastern and western countries discussed in the previous chapters of this book and the countries of the continent of Africa?

One, the countries within the continent of Africa differ enough on the continuum that we cannot universally say that all African countries have a similar cultural profile.

Two, the following countries have a common profile:

- Tanzania
- Kenya
- Zimbabwe
- Botswana
- Ethiopia

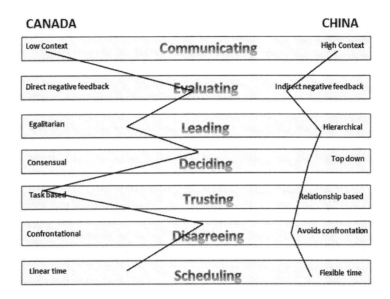

CANADA   CHINA

Low Context	Communicating	High Context
Direct negative feedback	Evaluating	Indirect negative feedback
Egalitarian	Leading	Hierarchical
Consensual	Deciding	Top down
Task based	Trusting	Relationship based
Confrontational	Disagreeing	Avoids confrontation
Linear time	Scheduling	Flexible time

Thirdly, their common profile is **similar** to China's in the following areas: **Communicating, Evaluating**, and **Deciding**.

Fourthly, the African countries are **different** than China's profile in:

Leading (egalitarian - hierarchical)
Botswana's profile is similar to China's, the other four African nations are slightly more hierarchical.

Trusting (task Based - relationship based)
All five African nation's profiles are slightly more relationship-based than China's.

Disagreeing (confrontational - avoids confrontation)
Kenya's profile is slightly more confrontational than China's, the other four African nations have similar profiles to China

Scheduling (linear time to flexible time)

The profiles for all five African nations are slightly more flexible time oriented than China's profile.

Although immigration to Canada from the African nations is not as significant in numbers as immigration from India, Pakistan, Philippines and China, it is useful to understand the business mindset of these new Canadians.

27
CONCLUSION

Common sense
Definition: *is a basic ability to perceive, understand, and judge things, which is shared by ("**common** to") nearly all people, and can be reasonably expected of nearly all people without any need for debate.*

William Glasser, an American psychiatrist and developer of reality therapy and choice theory, declared that all behaviour is purposeful. It is our best attempt at the time, given our current knowledge and skills, to meet one or more of our five basic human needs. It is the general motivation for everything we do.

Our five basic needs are:

1. **Survival** - This need is a physiological need, which includes the need for food, shelter, and safety. Because we have genetic instructions to survive, not only as individuals but as a species, this includes the need

to reproduce.

2. **Love & Belonging** - This need and the following three needs are psychological needs. The need to love and belong includes the need for relationships, social connections, to give and receive affection and to feel part of a group.

3. **Power** -To be powerful is to achieve, to be competent, to be skilled, to be recognized for our achievements and skill, to be listened to and have a sense of self-worth.

4. **Freedom** - The need to be free is the need for independence, autonomy, to have choices and to be able to take control of the direction of one's life.

5. **Fun** - The need for fun is the need to find pleasure, to play and to laugh.

We are all attempting to achieve these needs, regardless of our country of birth. The more different we are from those we work with, the more different our ways of fulfilling those needs may be. Their ways can appear not only foreign but even illogical.

There is little common sense in our world, if common sense means that the way I see the world will always match how those around me see the world. We no longer (if we ever truly did) live in a world where all things are common and where all things make sense.

To achieve communication, understanding, and ultimately success, we must reach beyond the surface. If we are trying to find a common bond with an employee or a colleague, the first step is to identify "how we see our world" and not assume that they see a mirror image.

Overlapping, innate and universal needs drive our motivations at an unconscious level but through conscious choice of communication and respect we can bring our worlds together.

NOTES

Chapter 3

1. *Witness for the Defense: The Accused, the Eye Witness and the Expert Who Puts Memory On Trial* (1991) Elizabeth Loftus and K. Ketcham. Elizabeth Loftus is a world-renowned memory expert and University of Washington psychology professor.

Chapter 4

1.*Culture and Point of View* (Proceedings of the National Academy of Sciences of the United States of America) Nisbett, R. E. and Masuda, T. (2003),
2. *Chung-kuo che-hsueh shi ta-kang (An Outline of the History of Chinese Philosophy)* Shih, H. (*1919*)
3. *Beyond Culture,* Hall, E. T. (*1976*)
4. *Individualism and Holism: Studies in Confucian and Taoist Values,* Munro, D. (*1985*)

Chapter 5

1.Vinland, Vinland," *The White Lantern*, Evan Connell, 1979.
Viking Discovery: L'Anse aux Meadows, Joan Horwood, St. John's, Newfoundland, 1985.
2.Dr. Helge Ingstad found at L'Anse aux Meadows in Newfoundland traces of iron nails, a bronze pin, soapstone spindle whorl of the type used in 1000 CE Iceland.
3.*Canada – A People's History*, Don Gillmore and Pierre Turgeon, 2000.
4."Land of the King of Portugal," *The Beaver – The Magazine of Canada's National History Society*, December 2002/January 2003.

Chapter 18

1.*The Culture Map: Breaking Through the Invisible Boundaries of Global Business*, Erin Meyer, 2014

Chapter 24

1. *On Time: How America Has Learned to Live by the Clock*, Carlene E. Stephens, 2002.
2. *Advice to A Young Tradesman, Written by an Old One*, Benjamin Franklin, 1748.
3. *Quoted in Keeping Watch: A History of American Time*, Michael O'Malley, 1990.
4. *Managing Cultural Differences*, Philip R. Harris, Robert T. Moran, and Sarah V. Moran, 2004
5. *The Dance of Life: The Other Dimension of Time*, Edward Hall, 1983

Chapter 25

1.*Clash, 8 Cultural Conflicts that Make Us Who We Are,* Hazel Rose Markus and Alana Conner

ACKNOWLEDGEMENTS

This is my ninth book. Hard to believe that I have had the blessing once again of a hardy group of friends and colleagues who have joined me on this journey as editors and sounding boards.

Thank you to my sister Laurelie, my husband Malcolm, and my good friends Carole Stepenoff, Carolyn Schur, Pat Dell and Alda Bouvier.

This particular book has been much improved by the specific edits of Will Roscoe and Dr. Shreedhar Jachak who gave me input on the Chinese religion and Hinduism chapters respectfully. Thank you.

BIOGRAPHY
JEANNE MARTINSON, MA

Jeanne Martinson, M.A. is a professional speaker, trainer and best-selling author who has worked internationally and throughout Canada. Since co-founding her own firm, MARTRAIN Corporate and Personal Development in 1993, Jeanne has inspired thousands of participants in her workshops and keynote presentations with her humour, insight and real-world examples.

Jeanne became interested in training while working for a Fortune 500 company in southern California. Back in her home province of Saskatchewan, she side-stepped into sales and marketing for ten years in the printing and labelling industry, where she took a $25,000 sales territory and grew it to $850,000 within four years.

Jeanne completed her Master of Arts degree in Leadership at Royal Roads University in Victoria, British Columbia, Canada. (Her graduate research focused on the differences and similarities of criminal gang leaders and corporate leaders). Jeanne also holds a Certificate in Organisational (Organizational) Behaviour from Heriot-Watt University (Edinburgh, Scotland) and is certified as a practitioner of NLP (Neuro Linguistic Programming).

As Managing Partner of her own firm, Jeanne delivers workshops and keynote addresses to government, associations and the private sector. Her most popular topics are leadership and diversity. As a Canadian bestselling author and strategist in workplace diversity, Jeanne's goal is to assist leaders in understanding diversity issues so they may attract, retain and engage their ideal workforce.

In July 1999, Jeanne released her first non-fiction book titled *Lies and Fairy Tales That Deny Women Happiness* which explores the myths that many Canadian women are raised with and which limit their ability to have happy relationships and fulfilling careers.

Her second book, *Escape from Oz – Leadership For The 21st Century* was released in October 2001. This book explores the parallels of the characters in the fable *The Wonderful Wizard of Oz* and our own beliefs about personal and professional leadership.

Jeanne's third book, *War & Peace in the Workplace – Diversity, Conflict, Understanding, Reconciliation* was released September 2005. This book explores how workplaces are becoming more diverse and how diversity may trigger conflict. The book illustrates how we have the choice of allowing conflict to spiral down into dysfunction or of taking charge, becoming aware and developing understanding.

Jeanne's fourth book was a chapter based on her graduate work in a larger compilation. Her research was published by the International Leadership Association in their annual journal (2012) as a peer-reviewed journal article (Leadership Lessons from the Criminal World).

Jeanne's fifth book, *Generation Y and the New Ethic,* was released Spring 2013. It gives concrete information about the four different generations found in the workplace today with a focus on work ethic and the motivations and values of Generation Y.

Jeanne's sixth book, *If it Wasn't for the Money,* is her first fiction novel and introduces her main character, Sam Anderson, a travel journalist and accidental murder detective. It was introduced in 2014.

Jeanne's seventh book, *Hemingway or Twain? Unleashing Your Author Personality,* is a book to help non-fiction book authors get their book completed with less stress, time and money.

Jeanne's eighth book, *Tossing the Tiara – Keys to Creating Powerful Women Leaders,* takes an update on the research from her first book, *Lies and Fairy Tales,* and adds information on gender gap, the impact on women of news media like FOX news and film.

Jeanne takes a leading role in her community, a dedication that was recognized with the Canada 125 Medal, the YWCA Women of Distinction Award, the Centennial Leadership Award (for outstanding contribution to the Province of Saskatchewan), the Athena Award, and the EMCY (the national Diversity award of Canada).

BOOKS BY
JEANNE MARTINSON

Hemingway or Twain?

Unleashing Your Author Personality

Written by Jeanne Martinson

On KINDLE and available in print through Amazon

Not making any progress on writing your non-fiction book? Too much advice from too many people but none of it seems to work for you? The first step to success as an author is to identify your Author Personality. With this knowledge, you can save yourself frustration, time and money.

After identifying the answers to the key questions that determine your Author Personality, apply them to the Ten Step Book Project Model to ensure completion of your book.

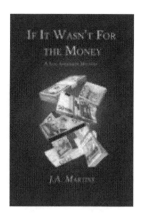

If It Wasn't For the Money

(Fiction)

Written by Jeanne Martinson under the name J.A. Martine

On KINDLE and available through Amazon

Sailing on a cruise ship to Alaska to discover unusual adventures to write about for her magazine, OOTA, journalist Sam Anderson gets caught up in the disappearance of a wealthy dining companion.

Who could financially benefit from the death of the heiress?

Travelling from the icy glaciers of Alaska to the steamy heat of New Orleans, Sam begins to tie up the loose strings of the mystery – but can she solve the puzzle before she too becomes a target?

(This is the first book in the Sam Anderson series. The second book, *Stay out of the Water,* is due out Fall 2017.)

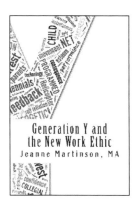

Generation Y

and the New Work Ethic

by Jeanne Martinson, MA

Available on KINDLE and in print through Amazon

Every generation has rebelled against the norms of the generation preceding it. This rebellion manifests itself externally in clothes, hairstyles, temporary and permanent markings. As time passes, often these visual distinctions are toned down or abandoned as that generation ages and begins to fit into mainstream work worlds, eventually falling for the tie and pantyhose cultural norms of the workplace. Many of today's Generation Y cohort members may yet desert their desire for T-shirts and casual attitudes as they progress in their careers and organizations.

Managers ask me frequently "When will Gen Ys will grow up, quit rebelling and get with the program?" Unfortunately for managers and co-workers everywhere, there is more to generational difference than rebellion and a desire to be different from the previous generation. Our generational identity is also about the beliefs and values that were developed in our growing up years. By the time we hatch into the workforce, our perspectives of others, work and the world are well formed.

So why are we talking about generational differences now more so than in the past? Why has this last generation upset the apple cart so significantly? Because it is the perfect storm between the end of the analog to digital shift and multiple generations in the workforce.

If you are a colleague trying to understand your multi-generational co-workers, a front line manager trying to get your youngest workers to show up and show up on time, or are a member of Generation Y and looking for ways to maximize your effectiveness and success in the workplace, this book gets to the heart of the generational differences issue, with minimal psychobabble and statistical navel gazing, giving you concrete information about the different generations with a focus on work ethic and the motivations and values of Generation Y.

Table of Contents

Introduction - Why is Generation Y so Different?

Chapter One - Defining the Generations

Chapter Two - The New Work Ethic

Chapter Three - The Loyal Traditionalists

Chapter Four - The Busy baby Boomers

Chapter Five - The Entrepreneurial Gen X

Chapter Six - The Newer Faster Generation Y

Chapter Seven - Why Occasionally None of this Matters

Chapter Eight - Why We Just Can't Get Along

Chapter Nine - Managing Generation Y

Chapter Ten - Workplace Strategies for Gen Y

Epilogue – A Letter to Leaders

Tossing the Tiara: Keys for Creating Powerful Women Leaders

by Jeanne Martinson, MA

Available on KINDLE and in print through Amazon

Women in leadership roles are good for business. When publicly traded companies have women in senior management roles, those organizations experience an average 47% increase of return on equity and a corresponding 55% increase of earnings. Women want to lead at the highest levels: when 1400 managers were asked if they had the desire to reach a top management position such as a C-suite role, 79% of women said YES. Yet women hold only 5.8% of corporate executive positions and 14.5% of board positions.

How do we reduce the gap between reality and aspiration? First we need to understand how fairy tale myth, media, and our history of communication have shaped where we are today. Secondly, we need to make different decisions if we truly want to create powerful women leaders.

Table of Contents

The Gender Wage Gap **13**

    Historical Inertia 14

    Education Doesn't Guarantee Equal Pay.................................. 15

    Occupational Segregation... 16

    The Caring Dilemma.. 17

The Sports We Play Matter **19**

    Rule #1 You'll Always Have a Coach 20

    Rule #2 Try Out 23

    Rule #3 There is Only One Quarterback................................ 25

    Rule #4 Shake the Winner's Hand 26

Disney and the Power of the Princess 29

Cinderella – There Will Always Be A Fairy Godmother **31**

Sleeping Beauty – One Day My Prince Will Come **45**

Snow White – Beauty Can Be Dangerous **54**

Beauty and the Beast – It Is Your Duty To Change Him **61**

Disney's Crippling Influence Continues...............................**71**

Disney Makes Us Want To Be the Perfect Princess **77**

    Self-Objectification 78

    Over-sexualisation 79

    Who Is In Charge? 80

Make Different Decisions **81**

Choose Media That Supports Female Representation 83

Choose An Employer With Grit 87

Choose A Gender Neutral Leadership Style **91**

Influence: Woman Talk 97

Insight: Write New Code 103

Self-Discipline: Even When the Going Gets Tough 107

Courage: Face the Music 111

Final Thoughts 115

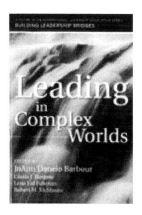

Leading in Complex Worlds

Chapter 8 – Leadership Lessons from the Criminal World – written by Jeanne Martinson

Available in print format from Wood Dragon Books

Released June 2012 by publisher Jossey-Bass, this collection of chapters from leadership experts and scholars is the annual peer-reviewed journal of the International Leadership Association. It contains chapters from fifteen authors, including a chapter by Jeanne Martinson titled "Leadership Lessons from the Criminal World" **which is based on her Master of Arts research project that compared criminal and corporate leaders.**

The other chapters include:

- Black Women's Political Leadership Development: Recentering the Leadership Discourse
- Soccer Tactics and Complexity Leadership
- The Role of Culture and History in the Applicability of Western Leadership Theories in Africa
- A Tao Complexity Tool, Leading from Being
- The Leadership of Dr. Jane Goodall: A Four Quadrant Perspective

Escape from Oz –
Leadership for the 21st Century

by Jeanne Martinson

Available in print and audio book at Wood Dragon Books

Available in KOBO and KINDLE eBook formats

This book explores the parallels of the characters in the fable *"The Wonderful Wizard of Oz"* and our own beliefs about personal and professional leadership.

The first part of the book explores the four cornerstones required to be an effective leader: courage, insight, self-discipline and influence over others.

The second part of the book explores how we can move out of our comfort zone to lead individuals according to their reality, skill set and knowledge base – with the goal of achieving trust and long term success.

This book, about the basics of personal leadership and leading others, is written to assist you in becoming an effective leader – whether you are leading an organization of two or two thousand.

War & Peace

(Diversity, Conflict, Understanding, Reconciliation)

by Jeanne Martinson

Available in print and audio book at Wood Dragon Books
Available at KOBO and KINDLE in eBook formats

Wonder why we can't just get along? Why we react to each other the way we do? Most conflict in the workplace comes from our differences – both our diversity in the big 'D' issues such as race, gender or ability but also diversity in the small 'd' issues such as values, marital and family status, age or thought processes. Diversity can be problematic and it can be wonderful. As individuals and organizations, we can benefit from the many perspectives that create the synergy to move an organization forward by leaps and bounds.

On the other hand, differences can bring conflict, toxic work groups, low morale, harassment, misunderstandings and employee turnover.

Many organizations adopt respectful workplace or harassment policies. But this isn't enough to realize the benefits of a diverse workforce or to minimize diversity-based conflict. We need to shift how we perceive and work with others. This book illustrates how we have the choice of allowing conflict to spiral down into dysfunction or of taking charge, becoming aware and developing understanding. It's all up to you!

Contact Info

Jeanne Martinson, MA
Diversity Strategist
Best-selling Author
Professional Speaker

Are you looking for in-house training on this diversity issue? Are you searching for a keynote speaker for your upcoming conference? Ask Jeanne to come and present to your organization or association.

Website: www.martrain.org
Mobile: 1.306.591.7993
Office: 1.306.569.0388
Snail Mail: PO Box 1216,
Regina, Saskatchewan, Canada S4P2B4

For more information on Jeanne Martinson, visit our website at www.martrain.org.

To receive Jeanne's monthly article series on diversity and leadership, email us at watertiger@sasktel.net.

Made in the USA
Charleston, SC
07 March 2017